D0130064

The Boy From
Treacle Bumstead

700040608976

The Boy From Treacle Bumstead

Ken Sears

With John F. McDonald

**SIMON &
SCHUSTER**

London · New York · Sydney · Toronto · New Delhi

A CBS COMPANY

First published in Great Britain by Simon & Schuster UK Ltd, 2013
A CBS COMPANY

Copyright © 2013 by Ken Sears and John F. McDonald

This book is copyright under the Berne convention.
No reproduction without permission.
All rights reserved.

The right of Ken Sears and John F. McDonald to be identified as
the authors of this work have been asserted in accordance with sections
77 and 78 of the Copyright, Designs and Patents Act, 1988.

1 3 5 7 9 10 8 6 4 2

Simon & Schuster UK Ltd
1st Floor
222 Gray's Inn Road
London WC1X 8HB

www.simonandschuster.co.uk

Simon & Schuster Australia,
Sydney

Simon & Schuster India,
New Delhi

A CIP catalogue record for this book
is available from the British Library.

This book is a faithful account of the author's experiences.
However, some names have been changed to protect
the privacy of certain individuals.

ISBN PB: 978-1-47111-357-4
ISBN Ebook: 978-1-47111-358-1

Typeset by M Rules
Printed and bound by CPI Group (UK) Ltd, Croydon, CR0 4YY

I would like to dedicate this book to the memory
of my beautiful wife, Marie –

also

To my children, grandchildren, great-grandchildren
and all my family –

also

To all the friends I've met along the way

Contents

The Hard Price of Chucken Eggs

I was born years and years ago, when there were bears and badgers and bogles in the woods round Hertfordshire, in a place called Treacle Bumstead, which was the name we gave to the village of Hemel Hempstead. The year was 1934. Stanley Matthews made his debut for England and Mao Tse-tung made his Long March in China and storms took away most of the topsoil in the Dust Bowl and the Wehrmacht swore an oath of allegiance to Adolf Hitler and the Three Stooges first hit the silver screen.

My father's name was Frank William Sears and he was a big-armed builder. My mother's name was Kathleen May Putman and she was a head-covered, hard-working domestic servant who was born on 1 August 1905 in Bovingdon, Hertfordshire. She was a small woman, my mother, less than five foot tall and pretty as a picture, and she worked in a big house in the local parish until she married my father. He was born in north London on 8 October

1908 and moved up to Hertfordshire with my grandparents when he was young.

The house we had in my newborn days was a small, two-up-two-down cottage in White Lion Street, Apsley End, and it was damp and cold and candle-lit. We had a kitchen range where all the water had to be hauled and heated, and my mother gave up her work in service to stay in her own little humble house and look after her growing brood of gobbling bird-mouths.

After learning the trade from his father before him, my own father started to work as a jobbing carpenter back in 1926, before he moved into White Lion Street with his wife in 1928. Times were hard and things like the General Strike and severe winters and shortages of work made things difficult for him. But he kept at it and struggled and strived and managed to start up his own little building firm in the good-weather year of 1929. He was a no-nonsense, hardy man and he looked big and solemn to my little self, when my bum was no bigger than a shirt-button. He probably knew very well he was going to have a goodly flock of children, just in case the whole leap and litter of us didn't survive the rigours of country life in the bleak winter months of growing up. And eventually he'd have to build us somewhere larger to live – somewhere we could all fit into and not have to be hanging out the windows to be able to put our coats and hats on.

I had three brothers and one sister before I was spat out – William Albert who was born in 1927, Peggy Iris who was born in 1928, David John who was born in 1930 and James Michael who was born in 1932. I came next on 21 January 1934, a night when snow came a-falling down in drifts from the dark, low-lying, crow-flying sky. Now, not many people can remember being born, but I can – every minute of it. I can remember the wind in the trees outside the window as I came a-kicking into the wilderness. You see, I didn't want to be here, in this world, I wanted to stay where I was, where it was warm and safe and tickety-bimble-boo. But I couldn't keep in there, my mother didn't want me to, so I was sent a-tumbling out onto the hairy bed-blankets.

I was but a year and a month old when my new sister Ann, who had no second name like the rest of us, was born in 1935. And after her came Richard Henry in 1936 and poor little Bernard in 1937, who died when he was but six months old. Mary Elizabeth was born in 1938 and Peter Frank in 1940 and, last of all, came Alec Alan, on St George's Day 1942. Only seven of us kids ever lived in the little cottage, before father built the new house, and there we all were, mother and father and three in the bed, three more in the cupboard drawers and one in the hall, wrapped up in tarpaulin. Like every large family, we had the good times and the rough and we shared them out between us so everyone got their fair measure of both. We children looked after each other – the older ones took care of me until it was my turn to look after the younger ones, stopping them from being bullied by other little buggers and taking them to school and making sure we all came home together and didn't get trampled on by horses or sat upon by big piglet-suckling sows.

As well as remembering being born, other things also come back to me from when I was but a little tiny lad – like being taken to my grandmother's house and her laying me on a tabletop to

change my nappy and me peeing on her nice new tablecloth and
her lifting me up by the legs and whacking me across the bare
bumkin for doing it. I ain't forgiven her for that to this blooming
day. I can't remember much about my grandfather, William
Albert Sears, except that he was a builder like my father and they
worked alongside each other sometimes, right up to when I was
sent away to reform school. My grandmother's name was Ellen
Howe and she was a domestic servant like my mother after her.
She was employed by the Reverend Arthur Durrant, who came
from a long line of reverends, all called Arthur, and who wore the
knee-breeches and black stockings of religious men of earlier
days. He liked to make the sloe-gin for the Christmas tidings and
sometimes you could see him skipping along in the lanes like a
little boy.

I know very little about my mother's family, except for her
three bachelor uncles – George, Albert and Fred. They were
farm labourers and lived together in an old country house in the
tiny hamlet of Bovingdon and my parents lived with them for a
short time during the hard winter of 1927/28, which lasted well
into March that year. You see, my father was out of work and not
able to find the ten shillings a week for the rent of the two rooms
in which he was living with my mother, so the uncles took them
in until things improved. The only source of lighting and cooking in the bleak bachelor house was candles and paraffin lamps
and an open fire. Gas mains had been brought to Bovingdon, but
the uncles refused to have it in their house and, even when my
father persuaded them it wouldn't cost anything and neither
would it blow them to Abaddon and back, like they thought, he

still had a hard job persuading them. And even when he finally did, they wouldn't light it if neither my father nor mother was there – liking better to light up a paraffin lamp or a fire to boil a kettle. And when my mam or dad lit it for them, they stood well back, and when the gas went 'pop' after the struck match was applied, they ran for cover, holding on to their hair.

Later in 1928, my father found work and was able to afford to rent the little cottage I was born into and it was in a bit of a state when he moved in. They had no furniture, my parents, so they made a kitchen table out of one of the bedroom doors and supported it on one end with crude batten legs. The other end my father fixed to the wall, because he only had the two batten-crude legs and I often wondered why he couldn't find four. But I never asked him when he was telling this story, only listened dumb-eyed, like the good boy I was. The uncles gave them a couple of chairs and they collected other bits and pieces over a period of hardship, until the place was at least liveable in for a fast-growing family.

That was back when there was only two chavvies,[1] William Albert and Peggy Iris. By the time I came along, the cold, low-ceilinged, candle-lit cottage on the edge of the wildwood was getting too crowded with all us children gadflying around like blackface lambs and father planning to make mother have many more before he was finished. So he built us a new house with his own bare hands and called it Sunnyside and we moved in there in 1936. It had three bedrooms and gaslight downstairs, but only

1 Children.

candlelight upstairs, and we had one of them old kitchen ranges for cooking and water-heating and a proper tin bath in its own special room for the getting-off of the week's dirt on a Saturday night. The garden was over a hundred yards long and we kept a pig called Humphrey who ate offal and a goat called Gerald who ate my jumper and seven Belgian Blue rabbits that we thought were pets, but sometimes one would go missing and mother always told us it escaped, but it never. It was slipped into the stew. And chickens and bantams for eggs, and father would kill and pluck an unlucky one on Christmas Eve. My picture-pretty mother planted carrots and potatoes and beans and other little bits and pieces for us to eat when times were lean and mean and we usually had enough in the bread baskets.

The house my father built for us was on a narrow rural road called Wood Lane End and we were hugged in between two farms. One was called Sherfields Farm and the other was Woodwells Farm and us children would work for the farmers in the long, red-sunned summer evenings, bringing hay by horse and cart and harvesting the corn and wheat and picking the spuds when the green stalk-leaves turned yellowish, and mangles and fruit when they were ripe and the pea-green pods and all the other stuff that farmers did by hand back then. When Michaelmas time came round, we'd help put fencing up round the corn ricks and, as the threshing engines got down to the bottom of the ricks, rats and mice would run out and it was our job to kill them with sticks and we'd be running all up and down and bumping each other over, with the snapping Jack Russells and the snarling fox terriers beating us to it.

And we got paid sixpence for their tails.

When the war had been going for a bit, the farms had POWs working on them. They were mostly Italian, but a few Germans as well, and they wore yellow tunics and had diamond patches on their backs and they were guarded by soldiers with guns who sat round smoking all day. They couldn't speak English and us kiddiewinks couldn't speak Italian nor German neither but, even though fraternisation was strictly forbidden, we managed to communicate with our hands and our smiling faces and our freckles and we half-inched cigarettes for them from the soldiers, when they weren't looking, and kicked a ball or two in their direction. They lived in tents at first, in a place called Batford, which was a few miles from where I lived, until the government built huts for them to have a roof over their heads. And they seemed like ordinary men to me – men like my father and grandfather, and not the 'orrible fang-toothed devils I was led to believe.

But before then I started at school. I was only four and it was like when I was being born – I didn't want to go. I wanted to stay with my mother and be safe and not be like a little waif being bullied by the winds and the rain and the bigger kids and the other things my brothers told me happened out there in the growing-up, shin-kicking rough place. But, like being born, I had no choice in the matter. My mother took me on the first day, the three-and-a-half miles on foot to the stone-built schoolhouse and the three-and-a-half miles back afterwards with my older sister, Peggy. It was called Queen Street School and it had been built back in the nineteenth century and had three classrooms. I can only remember one of the teachers and that was Miss Hoggett the music mistress. I remember her from the times I was kept back for being a bad boy and missed walking home with my brothers and sister. Miss Hoggett always gave me a lift in her little red Austin Ruby.

In 1940, I was transferred to a new school in Leverstock Green and it was a bit better than the old one, with bigger class-rooms and newer desks and sandbags stacked up by the doors and windows to stop the shrapnel from the German bombs that never fell on us. Mr Ayres was the headmaster and his daughter took the Sunday school class at the weekends. Miss Hoggett came with me from the old school and I wondered if it was because she was afraid I'd be left behind again and wouldn't be able to find my way home in the smoke-curling winter evenings. But the real reason was because the old school was being knocked down to make room for a cow-barn and nothing at all to do with me. They gave us a big spoonful of Virol in the morning when we came in to strengthen our bones and make us grow into good people. It was malt extract or bone-marrow or some other such thing and it had one of them tastes you either loved or hated – there was no room for nothing in between. I loved it but my sister Ann had to hold her nose.

In the middle of the morning we all had a half-pint of full fresh milk from the local cows and another one in the middle of the afternoon and school dinners in between, with wooden knife-and-fork held tight in each hand and thumping the table when it was late. Food was scarce in the war years, so we ate whatever was served up and sometimes it wasn't all that much. But the thing is, we never had no other nosh to compare it with, so we didn't know whether it was all that much or not – and that stopped us complaining. The lessons were reading, writing and 'rithmetic and a bit of history for the whys and wherefores of what was happening and what had happened to make it happen and, before that, what caused the thing that happened in the very beginning. And sometimes the geography to teach us where we were and where other places were, just in case we ever got to go anywhere when we grew up – like Lilliput or the Lakes of Pontchartrain. We also got to do a little bit of digging and weeding in the school garden, so we knew how things grew and when, and we half-inched the odd gooseberry and red-gudlo[2] when the teachers weren't looking.

People were being moved out from the cities during the war, because of the bombings and all hell breaking loose, and they sent the Finkel family out to stay with us from London. They came from the East End and they stayed six months. They were German-Jewish people and there was Mrs Finkel and her son, Raphael Finkel, who was six, and her daughter, Efrat Finkel, who was two. The father wasn't with them and they never said why not, nor where he was, and we never asked. They were poor people and they lived in our front room, in a makeshift world. Mrs Finkel cooked gefilte fish in our kitchen, which was stuffed with onions and eggs, and this smelled strange to us and my mother didn't like it. She also cooked red cabbage that she got sent out from London with her food allowance and chucken soup

2 Raspberries.

with balls of fat floating on the top. They never ate pork and we wondered why – not knowing in our ignorance of most things that they considered the pig to be impure, because it don't bring up its cud and the Hebrew Bible says so. My mother, as you know, worked in service and anyone who worked in service was very particular about things like tidiness and trimness, so there was a lot of tension between her and Mrs Finkel and us kids weren't allowed to mix much neither.

In those dark, bomb-dropping war days, country people were suspicious of strangers – and the people of Treacle Bumstead were more suspicious than most and a close-knit bunch of hilly-billy-hayseeds to begin with. They became downright hostile once the war started, and that included my finger-wagging mother. My father went into the army right at the beginning and was evacuated from Dunkirk in 1940, and he was away from home when the Finkels came to us. My mother didn't want the Finkels, but she had to have 'em because the government said so. The kids slept on the sofa in the front room and Mrs Finkel slept on the floor. The little girl used to wet the sofa, which was riddled with maggots, and neither of the kids went to school like us. We used to complain to our mam but she just said, 'They're Jews,' and that was the end of it. We couldn't understand why Jews didn't have to go to school and us ordinary old Church of England kids did.

We weren't allowed in the front room for the whole time the Finkels were there. That was the kind of peasant-minded prejudice there was for people who were having it hard and who we knew bugger-all about. But, just like school dinners, we never knew no better. We just hated the Finkels because they were 'German' Jews and we knew what Germany was doing to Britain, not what Germany was doing to the Jews. So the Finkel family kept themselves to themselves and hardly ever came out of the den they made in the front room of our hand-built Sunnyside house. We saw the kids sometimes looking through the window and we stuck our tongues out at them, but they never stuck theirs back out at us. We saw off the Luftwaffe in the Battle of Britain, and after the worst of the Blitz was over the Finkels went back to London.

We never saw them again.

Another family from the East End called the Wheelers were boarded out to Mrs Harding who lived up the lane from us. There were three boys – two were called Johnny and Ron and I can't think of the third lad's name. We made friends with them because they weren't Jews like the Finkels; they were wild kids who'd never seen an apple on a tree before and they got up to all sorts of mischief – like scrumping and snaring rabbits and bird-nesting and running the sheep all over the low hills of Hertfordshire. We rambled everywhere, us and the Wheeler boys, back in them long dew-falling days. We ran and skipped and climbed and scraped knees and split nails and they learned from us hayseed boys what wild thorn-bush fruit to pick and what nuts were sweet and what mushrooms to eat and on no account to touch the toadstools nor the hemlock nor the red berries that the birds ate. I was sorry to see them go back to London when they did and I know they were sorry to go.

At the end of 1941, America joined in the war and there was

thousands of GIs stationed in and around Hertfordshire – mostly in Bovingdon, where they had an airfield that wasn't far from our house. The Yanks used to say things to me like:

'Hey, mister, have you got a sister?'

And I'd shout over:

'Yes, chum, if you've got some gum.'

And it was a rare time to be a back-chatting boy, spitting in the lily-ponds and making catapults from Y-shaped sticks and tickling trout and bare-legging through the bluebell coshes[3] and whistling made-up tunes. It was a long-ago, light-footed time.

In 1943, I was caught stealing three chucken eggs and accused of killing the eggs' mother. But I didn't do it, your honour, honest to God. Me and my younger brother, Dick, went out in the fields around 6:00 a.m., like we'd do sometimes, looking for eggs that the chuckens laid in the meadows and hedges. The chucken was dead when we were passing by the coop and I thought the eggs might starve to death without a mammy, so I took them with me to give them a good home. The live chucks were a-squawking like mad and the man who owned the coop came a-running out and Dick was only six and couldn't get away as fast as me, so he got grabbed by the scruff. I ran off home. The bloke was called Dr Hedress and he worked for the government, even though nobody knew what he did for them down in London. But he came round our house with Dick and a policeman and my mother let them arrest me, because she had respect for the laws of the rich and ruthless drummed into her when she worked in service. Dick

3 Cosh = copse.

got let off, on account of his young age, but the copper took me down to the station on the crossbar of his bike and put me in a cell.

My father was told and they gave him a day off from the army and he came down to the police station and got me out. But a couple of weeks later I was taken back to the local magistrates' court in the Old Town Hall, Hemel Hempstead, and charged with the stealing of the eggs and the killing of the chucken. I pleaded not guilty, but I had no solicitor nor barrister to stand up and speak for me and my mother wasn't allowed to do it neither and my father was gone back to his barracks. Hedress testified that I was a thief and the magistrate believed him and sentenced me to go to reform school – or approved school as they were sometimes called – for five years. Before he passed the sentence, he turned to my mother and said, 'Mrs Sears, you have so many children, we'll put your son away to relieve some of the burden on you.'

I was nine years old at the time.

They took me straight to Boxmoor Remand Home in Treacle Bumstead. It used to be a mental hospital before the war and it was now a place for unruly boys like me to be taught a bit of manners. The masters were Mr Edwards and Mr Wally, who retired from the Lancashire Police Force to come down and teach us southern kids a lesson or two in respect for our elders. The place was run like a military training camp and the daily routine was tough and regimental and no place for snivelling snot-noses. I was given a grey jacket and a hairy grey shirt and grey pullover that was made for someone six stone heavier and grey short trousers that chapped the cold legs and a square blue tie and black shoes. The boys in there were aged up to fourteen and I was one of the youngest. But I was a tough little bugger from a big family and I never had much trouble with bullying. We had a five-minute wash every week, with two boys to a bath, in at the same time. Lights went out early at night and went back on again even earlier in the morning and we were on the go from the time we slid out of our skinny beds – doing this and that and digging and dowsing and pulling and pushing and cleaning and polishing. But the one good thing about it was, the grub was a bit better than I was getting at home.

They kept me in there for three months.

There was a secret wing in the old mental hospital and we could hear a woman wailing and knocking the windows on the still, moon-shadow nights sometimes. The secret place was above the laundry room and us bad boys weren't allowed to go nowhere near the place. The rumour that whispered itself round the log-chopped fireplace of an evening was that a member of the Royal Family was being kept there as a secret mental patient. I never knew whether this was truth or tall-tale at the time and it was only years later that I came to hear about Nerissa and Katherine Bowes-Lyon, who were nieces of the Queen and cousins of Princess Elizabeth. These women were kept in Earlswood Hospital in Surrey, because they had mental problems, but were moved somewhere else for a while during the war, as a precaution. Katherine would've been seventeen at the time and Nerissa would've been twenty-four. Not much is known about them, because Burke's Peerage said they died and there's no record of any member of the Royal Family visiting them when they were in Earlswood. I'm not saying it was either one or t'other of those women who was kept in Boxmoor the same time as I was there, but it makes you think, don't it?

As well as working, we had to learn our lessons, just like we would at normal school, and they used the cane and the birch on us to keep us in line. But Boxmoor was only a remand house and, after three months in the place with the secret mental compartment above the laundry room, they sent me on to the National Children's Home Orphanage school at Farnborough, which was a bigger place, with five separate houses and big grounds round it. I ran away from there every chance I got, but they always caught up with me and brought me back and I was kept there for another two years. But I don't want to get too far ahead of myself here.

2

Bushels for the Tallyman

Like I said, Farnborough National Children's Home Orphanage was a big place – much bigger than Boxmoor and with its own grounds and sports fields and high walls and humbuggery. It had a long-standing association with the Royal Navy, because one of its founders was a seafaring man and its five houses were all named after sea captains. Mine was called Nelson House and the housemaster was Mr Hammond – the brother of Wally Hammond, the famous cricketer who captained England and Gloucestershire. They wrote on my admission slip that my father was always away and my mother was struggling to raise her other nine chavvies – and it was like the old magistrate said, they were taking some of the burden off her by sending me away. I was described as hot-tempered, but healthy – a bit wilful and a one for the swearing. And I was in danger of turning into a right little hooligan if left to my wayward ways.

Classes were large and we were head-hammered the usual

lessons and once, just after the war, we all went down to the Isle of Wight to spend two weeks under canvas for the sailing regatta at Cowes. For those of you who might not know, Cowes is a port and natural harbour at the mouth of the Medina river on the northern mull of the island. Hundreds of yachts were floated in, carrying reams of toffee-nosed twits with silk neckerchiefs tucked under their shirts and smoking pipes and laughing to each other like demented crows with the croup. But there was brass bands and a carnival and fireworks on the last Friday that frightened me the first time I saw them, because I'd never seen fireworks before and thought they were bombs like the Germans were dropping and I wondered why the soldiers didn't shoot the buggers who were lighting them up.

I learned how to play cricket and football and billiards at Farnborough. But that wasn't enough to keep me there so, after a year, I started running away. I mostly ran away with another chap called Lilly Bedford, whose real name was Brian, but he got called Lilly because he had blond hair and that got him the nickname 'Lillywhite'. Lilly was from the East End of London and was in for six years for stealing a loaf of bread and kicking a constable in the shin. Him and me just palled up – it was one of them things and I can't remember why. Maybe I saved him from bullies or something, or maybe we were both from big families and lonely for the loudness and unruly ructions of the homes we came from – and not used to the taking of orders from straight-backed reform-school screws. The thing about bullies was, I didn't like them much. If I saw any of 'em picking on littler kids, I just went straight up to them and belted them. Sometimes they tried to belt me back, especially if they was bigger, but I was slippery as an eel in a bottle of oil and could dodge and duck until they tired themselves out trying to catch me. Then I'd kick the clob-heads in the shin. Most of 'em decided after a while it was better to leave me alone and stick to boys who didn't take so much effort.

You could say I was the bullies' bully.

The screws were quick to recognise my talents and, along with the cricket and football and billiards, I also started boxing at the NCHO. We couldn't hurt each other with the 28oz gloves that were nearly as big as ourselves, but we learned the proper disciplines of the sport and I liked it and became a fairly nifty foot-shuffling, rope-skipping fighter. But it still wasn't enough to keep me stayed put. Anyway, Lilly and I were best pals and he was a wayward lad like me and, when springtime came and the weather started to warm up, we both got the wanderlust in our blood and the sound of the wide open spaces in our ears and we had to leg it away from the orphanage school and be off across the hills.

This wasn't as easy as it sounds. The school had a six-foot wall round it and we had to squeeze in behind the prefab games room, which was close to it, in the damp dark of the toe-stubbing, shin-scratching night. Then we'd have to work our way up with our backs to the games room and our feet against the wall. Up and up – one foot over the other and shuffle our backs along to the same level. Then another foot over and another back-shuffle till we got to the top. We'd drop down the other side into an alleyway and be off on our toes before anyone knew we were

gone. It'd be a couple of hours before they missed us and they'd
ring the rozzers and show them the file with our physogs. We
were easy enough to spot in the grey uniforms with NCHO
printed on the backs, so we'd get off the public roads as quick as
we could and into the fields and hedgerows. Sometimes we'd steal
untended bicycles and other times we'd trudge on foot as far as
we could before they caught up with us. We only ran away in the
spring and summer times, when the weather got soft and we'd
feel the wanderlust inside our souls. We'd hear the hills calling to
us and we'd have to be away over the wall as soon as we got the
chance to back-shuffle up it.

Nobody came to visit me from back home in Treacle Bumstead and I suppose it was because they couldn't afford to make
the journey. My father was in the army and my mother had the
whole nine others to look out for. I missed my family more than
you'd think, for a rough-necked wrong 'un. There was plenty of
boys in the orphanage school, but it wasn't like being back home
in the big family with my brothers and sisters. It was like you
were surrounded by other boys, but you were still on your own.
I went flying back home the first time I ran away, but the police
were there waiting for me and I got arrested and taken straight
back. That taught me to forget about going home until the time
came for me to get out legitimate like.

Being a big-city boy from London, Lilly told me about the
hop fields down in Kent where the cockney families would go in
summer and it sounded right tickety-boo to me. So, once we got
over the wall, we half-inched a couple of unguarded bikes and
rode all the way south to Sittingbourne. Now, it was a long way

from Farnborough to the bittersweet hop fields in them days – longer than it is now, and it took us four or five days to get there. We slept softly in churchyards and allotment sheds and we ate the vegetables the kindly cabbage-gardeners grew for us and nicked milk and bread off the unwary carts we came across. When we got to the hop fields at last, we got taken in by a family from London who let us sleep on the floor of their homely little hut. We just threw down a couple of corn sacks over some straw and it was so warm and welcoming we didn't need to be covered over with nothing – just the feeling of being free.

We worked for our keep and the mother of the family took the money we earned to pay for the food she fed us and the straw we slept on. Me being a born-and-bred country boy and used to the wild ways, I was able to make snares out of wooden pegs with wire looped round one end and nailed in. Then I'd knock the snare into the ground at the entrance to the rabbit runs, so their furry little heads got caught in them. The rabbits added a bit of meat-flavour to the family's dusty old diet and, if I caught a lot of them, the mother sold them to other families to make an extra few shillings for her poor, hands-worn self. Me and Lilly didn't mind that she kept the money, we were just happy to be free and full of summer feverment.

The hop plants were called 'bines' and they grew up poles that were arranged along drills called aisles that went on for miles and miles. The pickers worked in gangs and I picked the hops in a gang with the rest of the family who took me and Lilly in. The work was hard and the hours were long and you had to make sure no hop-leaves got into the bin otherwise the fat-arsed farmer wouldn't take 'em. A tallyman would shive round to measure what was picked and collect them in a poke, using a basket called a bushel. He'd give the family tally-sticks to prove how much was picked and the mother got paid according to how many bushels were in the bin. The 'tally' rate was usually about thruppence a bushel – that's three old pence and not new ones like now – and you could say if you worked it out with a wongling-stick that a thruppenny bit would be a fag-paper or two over one nice new-penny today.

I worked from six in the morning till six in the evening and I don't know how much I earned because I never saw none of the money – but a good picker could earn two quid for a sixty-hour week, that's if it didn't rip down with rain. It was harder to pick the hops in the rain, because the little strobiles got all slippery and it took more time to fill the big bin. There were hundreds of hop aisles, up and down, and the vines blocked out the sun until the clusters got stripped off, then the light would shine through like a revelation. We'd have a little lunch break in the middle of the day, when we'd eat the sandwiches our hop-mother made with big thick slices of bread that looked like they were cut with a chainsaw and, at the end of the day, my hands would be all chapped and my grey NCHO clothes would be filthy and my back and legs would be aching and I'd smell like a bottler in a brewery.

All the other kids in the hop fields were from the inner London boroughs and they thought I was the bee's knees, with my wild wisdoms and country cleverness, and me and Lilly would bring back apples and pears in the dark late-night when

they were fast asleep and they wondered where the fruit came
from when they woke in the light mornings. We became part of
the family we stayed with and we were two more mouths to feed
and two more pairs of hands to work the tall aisles with. And we
loved our hop-mother and she loved us like we was two of her
own.

We stayed in the hop fields for three or four weeks with the
lovely old London people and it was a fine and fancy-free time
and we sang songs round the campfires till the lateness of night
and laughed and larked like we'd never saw nor heard of the old
NCHO. We stayed there until all the hops got picked and the
aisles were sad and bare and sorry it was all over with. The family
couldn't take us back to London with them because they'd only
get themselves into trouble and it wouldn't be fair after the lovely
days they'd loaned us. When it was time to go, we kissed everyone goodbye and set off back to Farnborough on our borrowed
bikes. The nights were beginning to draw in and the weather was
getting colder, so it was time to go back and wait out the winter
for the next springtime to come round. We left the bicycles in the
same place we nicked them from and I wondered what their
owners must've thought when they saw them – never knowing
that they'd run away for an adventure with two wayward boys,
but were now back to boring reality. We climbed back over the
wall before the school woke up. Then we gave ourselves up to the
headmaster and got six of the best and lost all privileges for a
month.

We ran away many times after that, me and Lilly, gadding
across the fields and along the railway lines and hiding in the

National Children's Home Farnborough.
Nine years old. I'm second in the second row.

hedgerows and frightening the horses and cows and sheep and
nicking apples and eggs and being wild boys with the whole
world after us and trying to bring us back and lock us up in the
orphanage school and throw away the key and never let us see the
light of day again – for me just finding a few chucken eggs and
for Lilly borrowing the bread and kicking the constable.

What a terrible travesty!

The last time we ran away from the NCHO, Lilly and me,
was on VE Day. The war was finally over and we knew everybody would be celebrating and having a good time and we
wanted to be part of it all. It was 8 May 1945 and the weather was
bright and warm and I was eleven. Once we got out of the

school, we made our way down to the railway station and picked up a couple of used penny platform tickets. Nobody checked the tickets getting on, so we didn't have to worry till we got to Waterloo. In them days, most of the trains had no corridors, only six-seat carriages, so no ticket inspectors to worry about neither. If we did happen to be unlucky enough to jump a train with a corridor, we'd always sit close to the khazi so we could run in there if we heard an inspector coming. Either that or the soldiers would hide us under their seats – the trains were always full of soldiers during the war. Once we got to where we were going, we'd hand over the used tickets and run like redshanks – or if we didn't feel like legging it, we'd just wait until everyone was gone and then walk back up the tracks a bit and get through a fence or over a wall.

It was afternoon by the time we got down to London and, after giving the bandy-legged ticket collector the slip, we headed up west to Trafalgar Square. That's where the centre of all the action was – as well as Buckingham Palace, where loads of people were cheering the King and Queen. The only other time I'd been to London was when my father was on leave once and him and his mate Ernie Cox took me down there in his 1928 Morris Cowley. They went into a dark pub called Dirty Dick's in Liverpool Street, which I found out later in life was one of a chain back then. It was said the first Dirty Dick's pub was in Bishopsgate and was named after a seventeenth-century bloke called Dick Bentley, who owned a hardware shop and never washed himself again after the dreadful death of his fiancée on their wedding day. Some even say Charles Dickens found the character of Miss Havisham in *Great Expectations* from this. Bentley was supposed to be a bit of a dandy when he was a young blade but, after the wedding day, he never looked at a bar of soap again and lived and died in septic squalor. The pub people changed its name from the Old Jerusalem to Dirty Dick's and recreated the state of Bentley's warehouse, with cobwebs and dead cats and gungecrud. Then the dive was taken over by Young's Brewery and there was a chain of Dirty Dick's boozers all over London when I was a lad.

Anyway, my father and his mate Ernie Cox liked to drink in this particular pub and they took me in with them on that one time away. The bar was below street level and I was told to sit in a corner out of the way with a glass of lemonade and an arrowroot biscuit. It was, like I said, my first time in London and I didn't get to see very much then except the inside of a dirty down-the-steps coalbunker of a bar. But VE Day was different. This time there were thousands of people everywhere, singing and dancing and drinking and shoes and shifts and spotted socks – jumping and bumping and whooping and cock-a-hooping. There were parades and bands and bonfires burning on the bomb sites and all the pubs open and street parties with speakers rigged up and knocking out scratchy 78 records. Girls were kissing us and Yank soldiers were giving us money and gum and bottles of pop – more money than I'd ever seen in my life, and Lilly and me buying doughnuts from the Red Cross 'doughnut dollies' and other tarts and teacakes we were never used to eating. There were soldiers everywhere and flags and bunting and it was like Christmas in the summertime and us just strolling through the festivities and stuffing our faces and pockets with food.

Hordes of kids followed the marching bands under the union-jacked buildings and we tagged along, until something else distracted us and we were like two street urchins in our reform-school clothes, two thin grey spectres, moving through the colour of the occasion – on the edge of it, being part of it and not being part of it, unnoticed – riding the crest of the day. And if Fagin had been around, he'd have had us back to Saffron Hill to join with his gang of pickpockets. But the day grew late and all the kids gradually disappeared from the streets – except for me and Lilly. That's when we got noticed by the coppers. We stood out like two small grey blots on the search-lit landscape, conspicuous by our inconspicuousness, and it wasn't long before we were having our frayed collars felt by a couple of bobbies on the beat. We could've tried to run off, but we knew they'd have run after us and caught us – they wouldn't stop chasing us with their shrill-whistles till they did and we were so full up to belly-bursting with cakes and fizzy drink, we'd probably have pissed ourselves and had to sit wet-arsed in some cell for the rest of the night. So we admitted we'd run away from the NCHO and they frogmarched us to the nearest police station – after first taking what was left of our money.

But the cop-shop was full up with drunks and down-and-outs and pimps and pickpockets and there was nowhere for them to lock us up. They rang round, but all the other police stations were full up too, so they put us in a car and drove us west across the city, without telling us where we were going. We thought they

might be going to drive us straight back up to Farnborough –
until we saw a sign saying 'Wormwood Scrubs Prison' and the
car came to a halt outside the brown brick and towers of the
medieval-like gatehouse. The coppers handed us over to the
prison staff, who took us to a cell – unlocking metal doors every
few yards and banging them clanging closed behind us and all the
cons jeering and saying how they were picking on little kids now.
I was no sissy, but this place was life-out-of frightening for an
eleven-year-old. It was getting on for midnight and they gave us
a cup of tea with no sugar and a lump of horrible old brown
bread-pudding, with no currants in it – then they locked us in the
cell. I didn't think I'd be able to sleep, but I was so knackered
from the day, I went out like a light and didn't wake again till they
opened the steel door at six in the morning.

They gave us a jug of cold water to wash with and a breakfast of egg and fried bread and tea with still no sign of any sugar.
Then the coppers came for us again and took us back to the
NCHO in a police car. We went in front of the headmaster when
we got back. The usual punishment of six-of-the-best was admin-
istered and we lost all our privileges for another month. But they
knew it wouldn't stop us – the wanderlust would come over me
when I looked out the window and saw the blue sky and the wind
blowing through the trees and the thing that was inside me from
the day I was born would whisper, 'Ken, it's time to climb over
the wall again.'

So, they sent Lilly away to Redhill Approved School in Surrey
and they sent me to a scripture-strict Catholic boarding school
that I can't remember the name of now, but it was in nearby

Aldershot. I was there for two months and I wished I was back in Wormwood Scrubs. I didn't know anything about Catholicism and I was constantly being belted with sticks and leather straps and kicked and punched about by nuns and priests. I had to join the choir and practise three times a day and on weekends as well. I soon learned that it went easier for me if they thought I was toeing the line and, when they thought they'd cured me of running away, they sent me back to the NCHO. When I got back, Lilly was already gone and they'd decided to transfer me to the Red House Farm School in Norfolk.

3

On the Steppe of the Red House

R ed House Farm School in Buxton Lamas, near Norwich, was a school for boys from twelve years up to eighteen. As well as being a farm school, it was also a sporting school, and this well appealed to me. I was always a lad for the tournaments and things and I'd learned the rules of games like cricket and football and billiards and boxing at the NCHO, so I kept it all up – oh, and I also joined the athletics team as a runner. The 800 metres was my best distance, but I did cross-country as well and if you've ever seen that film *The Loneliness of the Long Distance Runner* with Tom Courtenay in the borstal, that was me – running and running and running. Instead of running away in a straight line, I ran round in circles and ended up back where I started. So you see, it wasn't all bad. These reform schools were teaching me the discipline of the sports field and giving me guidelines in team-playing, things that would help me later in life, when I joined the army and got sent over the seas to Korea.

But I'll talk about all that later.

They put me to work in the laundry to begin with and I didn't like it there at first. It smelled of steamed excrement and stale urine and it made me sick as a drunken parrot. But the place was run by two village women who were good to us boys and not as strict as the masters. I got put in there because I was only twelve, the youngest level, and there was just the two of us boys in the laundry, along with the women. My job was to take the wet sheets and clothes from the wash-troughs and wring 'em through an old mangle. One of us would feed them through and the other would turn the handle. We'd wring 'em on a wide gap first time through, then fold 'em and close the gap and put 'em through again and they'd be nearly dry before we hung 'em on the lines to finish them off. The day started at 6:00 a.m. with breakfast, then seven till nine in the laundry, then school from nine till four, then laundry again from four till six, then free time for sports and other stuff till dorm and lights out at 9:00 p.m.

The laundry was considered an easy enough job by the boys at Red House Farm School. But I preferred to be outside so, when they realised I was a country lad and knew a carrot from a cauliflower, they transferred me to the garden-produce store. Same as the laundry, it was just two of us young 'uns in the store itself, with a dozen older boys out in the garden. Mr Abbs was the agriculture master and he was a cross old coot if you didn't get your work done. My job was to sort and store all the vegetables and fruit that came out of the gardens. Most of it was for the school's own use and the surplus was sold at the local markets.

The gardens were horizon-huge – all of ten acres at the very least – and grew every variety of fruit and veg and herb and nut and fly and frog that would propagate in the cloud-temperate English climate. The gardens were separate from the rest of the farm and the working day was the same as the laundry day, only stricter – not so easy-going as it was with the women. But I did my work well, because I didn't want to get chucked out of the job. I didn't like being idle – time passed slowly when you had nothing to do and it was much better to be busy. We also got our pick of the stuff in the store and that was an added bonus and not to be sniffed at in them stomach-hungry days.

Tobacco was grown out on the farm, but it was classed as part of the garden produce. It grew sunwards in the fields and needed dry warm weather to thrive. We picked the leaves in mid-September and I remember them being huge – big as blankets. They had to be really golden-brown before we could cut 'em with shortened, blunt-worn bagging hooks. Then they were packed into wooden boxes and a horse and cart came along and took 'em back to the big sheds to dry out completely and stop 'em from rotting before they got sent over to Ipswich to Churchman's Tobacco company, to be made into cheap English cigars that were smoked by bartenders and buckboard drivers and bank clerks.

After they found out I was used to working on farms in my freedom days, they sent me out into the fields to do the big boys' work as soon as they could. The man who ran the farm was Mr Swan and he was pleased to have someone who had a bit of experience, and not another city lad who didn't know a chucken from a chaffinch. In wartime 1940, the clocks weren't put back at the end of summertime, but were put forward another hour in summer to give the workers more time for the national effort and this went on up until 1945, when it all ended. It was called double summertime and, due to fuel shortages, they introduced it again in 1947. It meant the farmers had an extra hour to work with and they were growing two crops a year back then – harvesting the first crop by the end of July and the second in September or October. They rotated the crops as well and it meant plenty of work for us boys at Red House Farm School.

I thought the gardens were big until they sent me out into the farm itself – which was like being on the steppes of Russia. Two hundred acres of cornfields and wheatfields and kale fields and sugarbeet fields and grass fields for pastureland. We had fifty cows to herd and dozens of pigs to plump and chuckens to coop and ducks to drabble – anything that could be milked or bilked[4] to make money. The older boys did the milking in the morning, from five till six, and then again in the afternoon, from four till five, and the carts would come and rumble away the churns to the dairies.

Mr Swan liked things to be done his way and nobody else's. I was just a general gritknee to start with, doing all the rough jobs like shovelling the shit and working on the wold and picking potatoes and peas and fruit and mangles and swedes and topping and tailing and thinning the sugar beet. We'd be out in the fields before breakfast and then back in to do our lessons. After the schooling, we'd be back out again until it got dark – maybe ten or eleven at night during the days of double summertime and, in winter, we'd be bone-frozen to our wet underwear and have to

4 Conned.

plunge our hands chilblain deep into cold water to warm 'em up. And I mean *cold* water! We had to wear short hairy-leg trousers and thin shirts and scratchy jackets, with corn sacks cut to cover our heads and shoulders. Somehow the seasons seemed more like seasons back then – summers longer and dryer and winters frostier and clearer and the air better to breathe.

Anyway, there was a pair of Suffolk Punch horses on the farm. Now these beasts weren't your regular horse nor pretty little pony, they each stood over seventeen hands high and were solid as a Sherman tank. They were chestnut in colour and could get up a good gait on 'em. I remember that same breed being described somewhere as being 'bright chestnut – like a tongue of fire against black field furrows, against green corn blades, against yellow wheat, against blue horizons', something like that – and they were truly beautiful creatures. They never had much of a feather on the fetlock, like the heavy horses I'd seen on the farms at home, and they were shorter and better built than the Clydesdale or the Shire and more suited to farm work than road haulage. They were hard workers and would pull a plough or boat-wagon or a timber carriage till they dropped.

Because I had experience with horses from the farms when I was younger, Mr Swan let me lead 'em round at first. Then he let me harness them and stable them and it wasn't long until I was in charge of them two horses – that was my job. One was called Prince and the other was called Princess and I loved them like they were my own family and, after they got to know me, I think they loved me too – as far as an animal can love a human being, that is. Though sometimes I think animals are capable of stronger and steadier love than a lot of so-called humans. But it was the best part of being at Red House – the horses. I'd take 'em onto the fields, riding one and leading the other, and rig 'em up and put 'em into the shafts for the ploughmen and drive the carts full of corn back in from the fields and, after the work was done, I washed them and brushed them and brought them apples – and they got to know me so well they knew what I was thinking. It got so that, even though I was only twelve, them two horses would do anything for me. This was a happy time for me, maybe the happiest time of the whole five years I was in the reform schools.

Then Lilly arrived.

He kept running away from Redhill, so they sent him to Red House Farm School. He came in wintertime and as soon as I saw him I knew I'd get the wanderlust again, and it would be just as the blossom came on the bough and the thrush began to sing in the springtime trees. I was captain of the cricket team by now and playing football for the farm school's under-15 side in the Norwich Lad's League and doing the athletics and boxing and, like I said, I was happy after a fashion at Red House and never ran away once – until Lilly came.

After the winter finally wore away, spring came skipping and, right enough, I ran away with Lilly again – for the final time. We mostly used the railway-lines when we scarpered. We knew, from the times we ran away from the NCHO school in Farnborough, that the workmen's sheds always faced north and were always on the left side of the tracks – don't ask me why, I never found that out. So, if we walked along the other side to the sheds, we knew we were going south, which was usually the direction we wanted

to go. Sometimes we'd break into the sheds and kip down there
for the night. We'd light a little fire to keep us warm and be gone
by early in the morning, before any railway blackie or broke-
knuckle or bugslinger came round and caught us. Other nights
we slept in churchyards and we were right in thinking this would
be the last place anyone would look for us – because they'd be
scared of ghoulies and ghosties and pink elephants.

When we ran off this last time, we were kipping in Peter-
borough churchyard behind a big gravestone and this Yank
soldier and his girl wandered in, all a-kissing and a-hugging and
a-lovey-doveying. They got down to it on the grass next to our
gravestone and the noise they were making woke us up. We neck-
strained over the gravestone to see what the racket was and, as it
happened, an owl hooted at the same time. The soldier looked up
and saw two scrawny heads looking down and it nearly scared the
bugger back into his trousers. The two of them grabbed up their
clothes and took out to running and screaming and we found the
fags they left behind and settled back down with a nice smoke,
before heading for the fruit farms of Cambridgeshire.

We lived off the land or, like I already said, nicked stuff from
private allotments and we drank water from streams or stole milk
and bread from delivery vans. This last time we stole a bag of
money from a milkman's dray and it had £1/12s/4d in it and we
bought butterscotch and acid drops and toffee and Turkish
delight and were happy as a couple of bug-eyed sugar-fiends till
the cash ran out. But our luck changed for the worse and we
never made it to our destination. The weather turned really nasty
and it bucketed down for two days on the trot and we were

soaked to the shrivelled-up skin. We got so wet we just gave ourselves up to the first policeman we came across and he took us in out of the bad weather to a dry cell, until they could arrange transport to take us back up to Buxton Lamas. Red House punished me real bad when they got hold of me. I lost all my sporting privileges and had to go back to being a shit-slinger on the farm and Mr Swan took the horses away too. Lilly got transferred straight away to I don't know where and I never saw that boy again – and I never ran off again neither.

In 1947, my sister Peggy died of tuberculosis. She was only nineteen, but she'd been in Ware Sanatorium in Hertford since she was twelve. I knew she was away in a hospital because she went in there in 1940, three years before I was sent to reform school. But I didn't know much about what was happening to her – until she died. I was thirteen and they gave me compassionate leave and a train ticket to go home and attend her funeral. I travelled down to Liverpool Street station in London, then across on the Tubes to Euston and a train back up to Treacle Bumstead. I walked the three miles from the train station to our house in Wood Lane End, carrying my little brown suitcase. And I burst out bawling like a babby when I saw my little mother waiting there for me on the doorstep.

'Never mind, son.'

That's what my mother said to me. It was the first time I'd heard her voice in four years.

'Peggy's in a better place. So, I suppose it's a blessing in disguise.'

But I didn't know whether she really believed that or not. Peggy was out of all her pain and people were more philosophical about death in them days – especially people who came from large families. You didn't have time to brood over it and life had to go on trudging the very next day. They laid Peggy to rest in the churchyard at Leverstock Green and she's still there. All the older people of my family are there too, but it won't do for me. When I die I aim to be buried in unconsecrated ground, because I don't hold no truck with religion, after the way them Catholics beat me up when I was but a boy.

The day after the funeral, my father and his best friend, Ernie Cox, took me back up to Red House Farm School in the Morris Cowley. They stopped at many pubs along the way for me to use the toilet – even when I didn't need to. It took a long time for them to come back out of each and every pub, so we could continue on our journey. What should have took us about three or four hours ended up taking all day and it was eight o'clock in the evening when we finally got there.

'You're late, Mr Sears!'

The headmaster was more than a bit cross and thought I'd had it away on my toes again. But my father gave him one of his serious looks and he said no more. Then dad kissed me on the cheek and left me with these few words:

'Behave yourself now, Ken.'

And he and Ernie left, to drive back the 130 miles to Treacle Bumstead.

I had another year to go before I could come home again.

4

Frogs, Putlogs and Brickie Togs

I was fourteen when I finally got out of the reform schools. By then, I was a bit of a handful, after being toughened up by the places I'd been and the things I'd seen and all the running away and roughing it. And I was already a bit of a hard case even before I got sentenced. It was Easter time when I got out and, the very next day, I went to work for my father's building firm as a general labourer. It was 1948, and things on the building sites of them days weren't what they are now, with all the high-viz and low-whiz and yellow hard hats and harnesses. Although my father was an all-round builder and could set his hand to anything in the construction game, by trade he was a master carpenter and I think he hoped I'd become a carpenter too – like him and my older brother, Dave. My other older brothers, Bill and Jim, were bricklayers and I don't think Dad wanted another trowel-tapper in the family. I was always a bit in awe of my father and I wanted to keep him sweet.

'Well, Ken, what would you like to be?'

'A carpenter, Dad.'

'Right, son, you can come with me.'

He told me I could start an apprenticeship in two years, when I turned sixteen. But, for now, I could be his labourer and learn as much as I could by watching him pitch roofs and fix stairs and lay floorboards. I hit my thumb more times than the lost-head nails and, after two days of my old man's shouting and a thumb like a throbbing red plum, I'd had enough of carpentry and said I wanted to be a bricklayer instead.

So my father told my oldest brother Bill to take me with him and that was it – my first faltering steps to becoming a brickie. Only thing was, I never laid a single face-brick for the next two years, just carried the hod and knocked up muck and wheeled barrows and loaded out and shouldered sand and cement bags and dug footings. Everything was done by hand in them days – and it was done the same way the generation before did it. For instance, you didn't just shovel sand and cement into a mixer as you would do these days, you had wooden boxes to get the gauge right every time – two boxes of sand with two shovels to a box, to one box of cement with one shovel to a box. That way, you got the perfect four-in-one gauge every time. If you were caught doing it any other way, you got a larrup round the lughole or a kick up the khyber. And all the bricks had to be soaked in hot weather and sometimes I wished I'd stayed with the carpentry, even if it meant listening to my father lecturing all the day long.

I was paid £1/5s in old money a week and I had to give the pound to my mother for bed and board and that left me the five shillings for myself. The first thing I did was open a savings account and put the five weekly bob in there because I was saving up for my first motorbike. You'll easily work out that this didn't leave me any money at all for beer or birds, but my brothers always paid when we went to the pub and I was a good dart thrower and could always win my beer ten times out of ten. And as far as the girls were concerned, I was working so hard I just didn't have the time or the energy for 'em, even if I had the inclination. You see, Hemel Hempstead was being built up from a rural village into a town and there was loads of work going round and, when I wasn't working for my father, which was five and a half days a week, I was moonlighting out as sub-contract labour to other firms on Saturday afternoons and Sundays. And this gave me all of another £3 to put into my weekly motorbike savings account.

Like I said, being on a building site was a dangerous day's work back then – much more dangerous than it is now. They weren't so crafty with the health-and-safety and anything went to get the job done and dusted and make the quick money. Bricklayers set up their own scaffolding, sometimes with wooden poles planted in beer barrels, sunk three foot deep in the ground. Either that or in forty-gallon petrol drums filled with earth – we even used old discarded cold-water cistern tanks for a few years on my father's firm. The ledgers were lashed with wire bonds that were full of snags and would cut blood-deep into your hands because you never had no gloves. The putlogs were four-by-two boards for walking along and sometimes they didn't have enough transoms, which were crosspiece scaffold supports, and got overloaded and the whole shebang would go splintering down and bring everyone along with it – men carrying lintels and hods and bricks and broken legs and all. Many blokes back then were killed.

I remember once when a big splinter of flying timber lodged deep in my father's eye and he couldn't see through the tear-swelling at all. So he went down the hospital and had it taken out with a pair of tongs and then went straight back to work, even though he was in a lot of pain and had a punctured eyeball. He couldn't see anything out of the eye for a couple of weeks, but he kept working and that's what you did if you had an accident – unless it was serious and you had bones broken or unless it was fatal and you were dead. Men came to work whatever, pretending there was nothing wrong with them because they didn't want to lose their job for a 'little' accident, and they'd work on with lost nails and deep cuts and broken toes and eye gashes and all sorts of injuries. Unlike other industries, the building game never had much in the line of union stand-together – a man who couldn't work was no use to a gaffer and he'd be gone and his job filled the same day by some other scab. There would be no injury or sickness pay and nobody could afford a legal case in the courts to prove negligence or cowboy corner-cutting against the contractor or sub-contractor. So they worked on – missing nails and blood and broken toes and all.

There was never any safety clothing neither. You went to work in a suit and shirt and tie and shoes and flat cap. Some people put spats over their shoes to keep 'em clean, because they were the only pair they had and they'd have to wear 'em to church or to the pub later. I got my suits from a second-hand

hock shop and sometimes from the army and navy store over in
Watford, but the older men always liked to look smart in pin-
stripes and always washed their shoes before leaving the site so
they could walk into a pub and not be kicked straight back out
again by the cheap-cigar-smoking barmen.

Summers were hot and hard, but winters were even worse.
You could work in snow and rain, but not in frost. We didn't have
heated huts to stay in, only a canvas elephant, and we had to sit in
it till the temperature got to a rising 34 degrees Fahrenheit, which
was two degrees above freezing. There was always a temperature
gauge outside the elephant and if we heard my father coming, we'd
go and breathe on it and get the mercury to go illicitly up so we
could start work to warm our cold hearts. Me being only fourteen
and the youngest on site, I was always being given the gofer jobs
and asked to get imaginary things like a bucket of putlog holes or
a set of sky hooks or a gallon of tartan paint or a headless
broom – while the others would be a-sniggering and a-snorting
up on the scaffold and watching me making a fool out of myself.
I was glad when I got a bit older and my younger brothers came
into the firm when it was their turn to grow up. Dick came as a
carpenter and Peter as a digger driver and Alec as a bricklayer like
me. There we all were then, all part of F.W. Sears & Sons.

But, generally speaking, I always liked working and it wasn't
too bad with my brothers, because we all got on well together and
nobody gave it the big 'un and we were alright and knew the pack
pecking order. And I never got into no trouble – as long as I did
what I was told.

Two years stole by quick enough and I soon became sixteen.

I'd already sent away for a provisional licence to ride my motorbike and I signed the indenture papers and began to serve my time as an apprentice bricklayer. It was a five-year apprenticeship – part on-site experience and part theoretical stuff at Watford Technical College. But I rarely got to the college because of the long working hours and I think my father might have had an encouraging word or two with the academics while waving a five-pound note in front of them, because I passed all the stages without actually having to be there. My wages went up to thirty shillings a week, so I could afford petrol for the motorbike I bought with my savings. It was a Royal Enfield 125 and I still remember the number plate – LOD 138. My licence came through before the bike, so I was able to ride it straight out of the delivery truck and away in a cloud of exhaust smoke.

It was 1950 and I felt like Johnny Jump-up – two-star petrol was 2s/4d a gallon and I was free as a bird. I never told no one about the bike and kept it under wraps after I test-drove it all over the Hertfordshire hills. Next morning and my father was getting us all into the old Morris Commercial one-tonner that he'd converted into a builder's truck and I usually had to sit on the back with the younger 'uns, in all kinds of weather.

'Jump up on the truck, Ken.'

'Not today, Dad.'

'Why not?'

I pulled the tarpaulin off the hiding bike and it was like I was a magician pulling a rabbit out of a top hat.

'De daahh!'

'Where'd you get that from?'

'I bought it.'

'Where'd you get the money from?'

'I saved it.'

So, from then on, I could spend an extra half-snoozehour in bed in the morning and still pass the truck by the time it got close to the site.

In the spring of 1950, my father called all his sons together and told us the firm of F.W. Sears was struggling and we all had to pull even more weight than we already were to keep it going. He suggested with a serious face that we each could contribute a pound of our wages to the cause and he would match this with two quid of his own. This meant seven quid would be saved by us boys each week and the money put into a deposit account with Barclays Bank, in the names of my father and my oldest brother Bill. No withdrawals could be made without joint signatures and the money would keep the business afloat and we'd all be shareholders and self-made higoshiters[5] and get back more than we put in when the hard times passed. None of us sons saw any problems with this honest-injun proposal and, anyway, we knew by working a little harder and a few more hours each week, we'd never even miss the pound we contributed to this worthy cause that could, in later life, make us wealthy as walruses. But things don't often turn out the way we want them to and, while some of the sons eventually reaped their rewards, I myself was left way out on the cold commercial shoulder when the time came to divvy up.

5 Someone who thinks their turds don't stink.

But I'll explain all that stuff later.

I think it was also 1950, or maybe 1951, when my grandfather, William Albert Sears, ran off to New Zealand with another woman who was a fair few years younger than his grisly old self. This caused a bit of a scandal both here and in New Zealand, when the dour old Scots Presbyterians on the North Island found out the woman he was living with over there wasn't his wife. Her name was Mrs Wright and I think she was still married as well and left her husband for my philandering grandparent, although God knows why – he was sixty-seven years of age. No one in the family ever saw the old bugger again, but we did see Mrs Wright, seven or eight sour years later. She told us they had to leave New Zealand in 1956 because of the scandal of not being married and poor old William Albert lost his job and was ostracised by the holier-than-thou folk. He died of cancer in Colchester in the same year and bequeathed his body to the School of Anatomy in Cambridge, for use in cancer research. So, there wasn't even a grave or a churchyard marker to remember him by. I only tell you this because I always saw it as interesting that my grandfather was a bit of a rake and a rambling boy and my father was as straight-laced as a spinster's bodice. The randy-old-goat gene must have skipped a generation.

Anyway, getting back to the building sites – I worked hard and learned quick and knew that if I didn't face the frog[6] upwards at all times I'd get a belt round the back of the head, and by the time I turned seventeen I could lay 1,000 face-bricks in a day and

6 The indentation on one bed of a brick, for holding the mortar.

back it up with the same amount of rough common bricks or flettons. The more experienced men could lay between 1,500 and 2,000 but, when you consider the average nowadays would be about 400, I wasn't doing too bad for a bald-arse. We started work at 7:30 a.m. and kept at it until 6:00 p.m. and sometimes even later. Saturdays was from 7:30 a.m. till 12.30 p.m. We never missed work for hangovers or hay fever or lung-ache or lazyitis and we worked fast, faster than any other firm I knew of. Don't think I'm bragging or boasting or thatlike, because I wouldn't, but this one time we were building a bungalow in a place called Cupid Green – we started digging the footings out at 7:30 a.m. on a Friday and by 6:00 p.m. we'd concreted them in and built the brickwork up to dampcourse level and concreted the oversite – and there was only the three of us working, my oldest brother Bill, myself and a last-legs labourer. On Saturday morning, we took the brickwork up to plate high and bedded the plates on. We went home at 2.30 p.m. and Bill told my father it was all ready for him to put the hip-roof on. Dad didn't believe us and took his tools up to the site and by nine o'clock that night, the roof was finished. On Sunday, the tiler felted and battened it and Dad fixed all the internal frames. The new owner was able to move in after only twelve days.

That would never happen today – no way, José.

Despite him always pleading poverty, my father's firm had plenty of work during 1950 and 1951, and he only took on what we could handle as a family, with two or three other men from outside the fold. That way, Dad could keep an eye on everyone and make sure we were all pulling more than our weight. My father's mantra was that hard work and thrift made for a better life and he expected a lot for the wages he paid. I suppose you can't blame him, after the many hardships he'd been through in his life, trying to build up his little builder's business and he was making sure nothing was going to jeopardise it – especially no extravagance by the more irresponsible of his seven sons. Bill, the eldest, was his favourite boy. He was a bricklayer with a work ethic like my father – work as hard as Hagar and take as little as Lot out of the business, in case hard times might be a-coming round the corner. The rest of us subscribed to this because, after all, we had a share in the stockholdings – didn't we? We were paying our pound a week into it and it was ours. The Treacle Bumstead town was a-growing and we branched out from houses to shop premises and conversions and extensions and worked for the Borough Council and Hertfordshire County Council and the Crown Land Commissioners.

Things were going well for F.W. Sears – and Sons.

But in 1952, two years into my apprenticeship, National Service came and interrupted my journey through the building trade. I was eighteen when I went in and I'd be twenty-three years old by the time I came back out again and got my bricklayer's certificate. I could've had a two-year deferment, but I wanted to get it over with as quick as possible and get on with my life.

So I went into the army.

5

Going Barmy in the Army

You could say in a way the military was in my blood, because my Uncle Alec – on my father's side – went into the Royal Navy in 1937, when he was just a fidgety lad of fifteen. He signed up for twenty-two years and rose to the rank of Chief Petty Officer. Some would insist that's nothing much to be writing home about, but he saw a lot of action in the Pacific during the war and, when he was stationed in Hong Kong harbour afterwards, he was given the job of driving King George VI around. The King got along with Alec so well, he wouldn't have no other driver no matter where he travelled to. And Alec would be flown to whatever country the King was in, just for the driving of him. Now, you could put that in a long letter, couldn't you?

Alec met and married his wife when he was out in Hong Kong. She was in the British Navy too and I think she might have been a nurse and they got together in the sweet-and-sour sunsets and fell in love. He left the service for some reason in 1948, the same year I got out of reform school, and joined the fire brigade first – and then the police force. He became a sergeant and was stationed in Hemel Hempstead when I was an apprentice brickie with my father's firm. You're probably wondering why I'm telling you about Alec and you might be saying me and him would never get on, him being a copper and me being such a rapscallion – but we were good mates because we understood each other. He knew what I was and I knew what he was – and that's good enough grounds for being on trustworthy terms. Ain't it? As well as that, Alec saved my bacon before I went to Korea and I'll tell you about that too.

But not now.

Anyways, King George VI died the same day I got a letter for my medical at St Albans Territorial Army Centre. I'd just turned eighteen and along with the letter came a travel warrant and a ten-shilling postal order to buy a razor and comb and lather brush – so I bought half-a-gallon of petrol, ten Woodbines and two pints of beer instead. But the army gives away nothing for nothing, as I soon found out. They paid us £1/2s/6d a week, and took the 2s/6d back for barrack-room breakages, even though there wasn't ever any such thing. Except on the rare raucous occasion. It was an army illusion – now you have it, now you don't – a special squaddie tax on the weekly pay packets of us poor conscripts. But, still, a quid a week in my pocket made me feel like a millionaire, considering I only ever had five shillings left out of the wages my father paid me, after giving the rest to my mother – and having to work all the hours in the daylong for it.

I joined the Bedfordshire and Hertfordshire Infantry Regiment, which was part of the East Anglia Brigade, on 17 April. It was a Thursday, as I remember, and I assembled at Boxmoor Station with John Wells and Henry Tovey and Dave Griffiths and Ray Hobbs – all from Treacle Bumstead – and Bob Wellings from Berkhamsted. We took the train to Leighton Buzzard and chatted and chuckled and changed there for Bedford. We arrived at midday and were met by two army trucks that took us over to Kempston Barracks and, as we drove in through the gates, the place looked more like a grim prison or a medieval castle keep than a training ground. It was built in 1875 and the rumour went round that it was supposed to be haunted by the ghost of a soldier who committed suicide there by shooting himself in the head – around the time of the Boer War. Apparently, a group of WRACs was billeted there and one of them saw a man covered in blood with half his face blown away. I didn't like the sound of that, to start with.

The first place they took us was to the mess hall for a feed of regular army rations, which wasn't too bad. I was never a fussy eater and didn't complain much about the grub, like a lot of others did. I was of the mind that if I had to become a soldier for a while then I might as well get on with it and get it over with, so I could get back to my real life. And, in a naive way, I was looking forward to it because my idea of a soldier was like I'd seen down in London on VE Day when me and Lilly ran away from the NCHO – like girl-kissing and loud-laughing and jig-dancing and chewing gum and having a great old all-the-time. But I soon got brought back arse-bumping down to earth.

After the grub they took us to the clothing store to be issued with our kit and caboodle. The fierce-face behind the counter assaulted me with his scowl.

'What size are you?'

'Dunno.'

'This'll do you.'

He threw some stuff at me and asked about my head. I said my hat size was 6⅛.

'No such size. Here's six-and-a-half, it'll shrink into you.'

The uniform looked like someone else had been wearing it before me – a much bigger man than myself – possibly Coco the Clown. And the boots were too big and too ugly and they gave me enough webbing to bridle one of the Suffolk Punch horses at Red House Farm and an old Lee-Enfield bolt-action 303 rifle that looked like it would be quicker to club someone to death with than shoot them.

We were then herded into the sleeping quarters with twenty-five steel-framed beds lined up on both sides, and we had to fold any clothes we weren't wearing and store them at the tops of the beds in a strictly particular square sequence that some failed mathematician with obsessive-compulsive disorder dreamed up, because we had no lockers or other luxuries like that. Socks top left and cellular drawers top right, this here, that there, and the other in the middle. Then the webbing – belt and gaiters and shoulder-straps and small packs and big packs and ammunition pouches. All perpendicular to the hypotenuse. Then our 'house-wife' kit – sewing needles and cotton and buttons and bows and then the razor and comb and lather brush and button brush and

Brasso and blanco – like small soldiers standing. At 'taps', we had to take all the stuff off the beds to get into them and place the abstract geometric arrangement carefully on the floor next to us. Then make the bed again and replace the sub-quadratic triangles on it in the morning. Now, to me, this was a ludicrous waste of my time and, once I was there for a while, I made up this cardboard frame that kept everything nice and neatly symmetrical. I also sussed out a system using another square of cardboard in between two blankets and my spare trousers in between two sheets to keep them permanently pressed. It worked well and I'd explain the process in more detail only you'd need a degree in algorithmic sequences to understand it.

Reveille was at 0600 hours, with the NCOs screaming:

'Hands off cocks and on socks!'

'Come on, out of your wanking chariots!'

This was followed by breakfast, then ablutions and an inspection at 0800 hours. There was a barrack-room checkup every morning and they'd count all the kit you had displayed on the bed and if anything was missing, stolen or the like, you had to pay double to have it replaced – one price for the new piece of kit and one for the lost piece. Another army tommy-tax. And, to add insult to injury, they'd check that your boots and buttons were shining like a shilling up a sweep's arse. A full kit inspection came once a week – on any day they liked and they'd change it around, just to catch us out. I was OK with this because I was already institutionalised from the reform schools. But I could hear these other eighteen-year-olds crying at night because it was the first time they were away from their mammies, and I shouted at them to grow up and shut up, so I could get some sleep.

It didn't take long for me to find out that the army didn't take kindly to upstarts and nonconformists like myself. Discipline was imposed, or should I say, inflicted, by the NCOs. These vindictives wore V-shaped chevrons on their sleeves – one V for a lance corporal, two Vs for a full corporal, three for a sergeant, three with a metal crown for a sergeant major and three with a cloth crown for a colour sergeant – and a regimental sergeant major had a crown on his lapel. They all demanded respect, whether they earned it or not, and they had great big tongue-full mouths and shouted at us all the time, as if we were bloody deaf. They never smiled and were always immaculately turned out – knife-edge-creased uniforms and buttons and buckles shining and boots polished so bright they could light up a dark room. They walked around like barking robots with broom handles shoved down the backs of their shirts and they rarely bent their knees, except to do a silly little stand-to-attention if a senior officer walked past. They made me laugh when I first got to Kempston Barracks.

But I wasn't laughing for long.

The first morning I was there, I was sent along a white-walled corridor with forty other new recruits to see the Medical Officer.

'Right, you lot, strip naked!'

We had to form up in alphabetical order and, me being an S for Sears, I was at the back end of the queue. It was cold in the corridor and it took a while for my turn to come.

'Stand to attention, soldier!'

The MO lifted my meat and two veg with his baton, then told

me to bend over and he looked up my bumhole and declared me fit for duty.

'Move on, Private Sears. Next man!'

Blimey, I could have told him that and saved the time. What he could see up my arse that confirmed my fitness, I'll never know. Next, we had to have our inoculations – six of them. Again, I was at the tail-end of the queue and they used the same needle for all forty of us. The thing was blunt as a spoon by the time they got to me and then I had to go back into the end of the queue for the next one. Six times round and six blunt needles. My left arm felt like it had been walloped with a pointless porcupine and it was swollen for a month of Mondays. But they told me I was underweight at 10st 3lb, so they gave me steak once a day for three weeks, until I reached the regulation weight of 10st 7lb, then the steak dinners stopped and I was back to the regular slop.

For the most part, the training consisted of square-bashing and shining boots and marching and rifle drill and more square-bashing and polishing brass buttons and buckles and badges and blancoing webbing and more square-bashing and more shining boots and more marching and more polishing – as well as that, we learned how to identify and address and salute the different ranks above us, which was every single one of them, as we were the lowest of the lowly. Rifle drill was usually early in the morning and, although it was springtime, it could be cold and sometimes misty.

'Get fell in!'

The drill sergeant had a limited vocabulary but, after a while, everyone knew what he was saying. He'd march us round and round, swinging the heavy old Lee-Enfields up and down and shouting words with elongated syllables – 'staaaand-aaaat-ease' and 'attennnnnn-shun' and 'quiiiiiiick-march' and 'abouuuuuut-turn' and 'companyyyyyyy-halt'. And, when it was all over, he'd scream 'dissssss-miss'.

It had to happen sooner or later and I was only four days into my National Service when I got my first seven days' jankers. This meant doing all the 'orrible jobs like cleaning the latrines on your hands and knees with the smallest scrubbing brush they could find, or painting a blue wall green and them saying they don't like it and painting it back the same sad shade of blue again, then gormless green again, then bullshit blue again, or the NCOs getting you doing their kit and washing their shorts and shirts so they lasted all day without going crinkly, or cleaning the officers' living quarters, or any other dirty and demeaning job the buggers could think of. And you still had to do your usual duties and be going till ten o'clock at night with all the other laughing-heads taking the Michael.

Humiliation was the required end result.

Anyway, I was coming back from football training this particular day and these three or four blokes were messing about with a motorbike, riding it round and round. Well, I couldn't resist no motorbike, could I – so I had a go, showing off what I could do and everything. I didn't see the sergeant coming, but the others did and they all scarpered and, when I turned the bike round on a stationary with the chassis and back wheel spinning like a jenny, I nearly knocked the scowler off his flat feet. I was put on seven charges and got one day's jankers for each – like I said, jankers was army slang for punishment if you were put on a charge, for those of you who've never cleaned a toilet with a toothbrush.

But it wasn't bad all the time. We had to learn how to strip down the 303 Lee-Enfield rifles and clean them and reassemble them, in readiness for the firing range. And this is where I came into my own. On the first day, I was expecting we'd be driven to the rifle range by lorry. But I was still naive and unused to the ways of the British Army – we had to march the five miles to the range at Caddington. It had to be done in an hour, with one ten-minute break for a gasp of breath and a fag and then back on our feet again. At the range, we were issued with five rounds of 303 bullets and told to fill our magazines but not to fit them into our rifles until we were lying in the trenches. It was raining, of course, on that first shoot, and the ground was muddy-wet and soaked cold. The targets were 200 yards away – six foot by six foot square, with an inner bull and an outer bull – anything else was a miss. Once we were lying in the squelchy trenches, we were told to load and, before firing, grip with our left hand and turn the rifle stock into our right shoulder – I can only imagine how difficult this must've been for the southpaws among us. But it didn't bother me. On the first command, we were to put one round in the spout and take off the safety catch. On the second command, we were to fire, then wait for the man in the butts to show our score.

'Fire!'

My ears nearly exploded and it felt like my shoulder had been kicked by a mule.

'What's the matter with you, Sears?'

'My shoulder's broke.'

'No, it's not. Grip your rifle properly. By the way, you scored a bull.'

The bull's-eye flag had been run up by the man in the butts behind the targets. How I did that, I'll never know. We were then told to fire our four remaining rounds at will. I shot three more bulls and an outer. It was the top score and I felt as proud as a peacock on a pedestal. I went on from this auspicious start to become a marksman on the rifle and Bren light-machine-gun. I was given a prize of money for achieving this – five shillings for the LMG and 7s/6d for the rifle. Not a bad little bunce, eh? I was also top marksman on the 800-yard range – running 200 yards and firing five rounds standing up, then running another 200 yards and firing another five rounds kneeling down, then running another 200 yards and firing another five rounds lying down. This wasn't all that easy, because I had to control my breathing by sucking in deep lungfuls before each shot – air up the nose cavity and hold it for ten seconds before hissing it back out through the teeth. If you didn't breathe right, the rifle went all over the place and could've shot the captain up the khyber. But I did good and was the only one to get it right from the whole intake of wet-eared NS men to the Bedfordshire and Hertfordshire Regiment.

The other thing I didn't mind getting mixed up in was 'milling'. The gloves and the ring regulations were just like boxing, which I was good at from the reform schools, but the rest was just a free-for-all. Everybody had to do it, it didn't matter if you were a country lad like me or an officer's son from shit-don't-stink-shire. Two at a time were selected and got into the ring and punched away at each other for two minutes. Then the bell rang and the next two got into the ring and this went on until everyone had had a go. The ones who couldn't box just lay down on the canvas as soon as they felt the wind of a glove come near them and the whole purpose of it was potential – they were looking to see who was NCO material. But I never wanted to be no corporal, even though I was a good boxer – I just wanted to get in and get back out with as little fusspotting as possible.

Competitions between barrack rooms were sometimes organised by the officers and you often had to get in the ring with lads who were much bigger brutes than you. But it didn't matter to me how king-sized they came, because not many of 'em were as good with the gloves as I was and they usually came off the worst for wearing the leather. They'd get in the ring and charge at me with both hands flailing and boots pawing at the floor like bulls in a rope-ringed china shop. I'd just step out of the way and let 'em run past like I was a foot-lightly matador. By the time they turned round and ran back at me again, they'd be out of breath and I'd let 'em have a left hook on the way past. That would slow 'em down and they usually had no defence to speak of and I'd just belt the daylights out of 'em until they dropped down on the canvas.

Other than the jankers every other weary week, I didn't get into much trouble on basic training – except for one time. This corporal called Johnson had it in for one of the boys whose dad was a sergeant major during the war. The corporal had served under the boy's old man and had obviously had a hard time from him. The boy wanted to go into the same regiment as his dad, which was the Beds and Herts. Unfortunately for him, Corporal Johnson was still there and looking for a day of reckoning. He ordered three of us to grab this boy and strip him arse-naked and throw him into a bath of cold water, and then scrub him with the hard hobnail brushes we used for taking the skin off the floors. The boy was screaming and a-kicking, and I didn't think the corporal would actually go through with it – I thought he only wanted to frighten the boy and make him cry and that would be enough for him to shake a faraway fist at the father. But when the other two with me started to apply the hard-bristled brushes to his bare skin, that was enough for me. I turned round and belted the corporal straight in the mush and turned his grin upside down. He didn't think much of it and he had me arrested and I was hauled up for hitting him – but it stopped his bullying.

The corporal lost a stripe and he kept clear of me after that.

There wasn't much R&R during the months of basic training and it was four weeks before we were allowed into town on a weekend pass. Instead of sinking down into the pubs and fleshpots of Kempston, I went home on the train and brought my motorbike back with me to the barracks. Any weekend pass I got after that, I'd just ride the bike on home and take my time about it too because, if I got there too early, I'd only have to go to work with my father on the Saturday morning. I was eighteen back then and you'd think I'd be more interested in going into town and getting stupid drunk and stumbling after the girls than going back home and having to work like a horse for my heartless father. But, even with a quid a week in wages, it wasn't near enough to be going on the pints and the pull all weekend and then feeling lousy on Monday morning when you had to go back square-bashing again. Didn't seem worth it to me.

After the eight weeks were done, we were given four weeks' leave and I went home on my motorbike and straight back to work for F.W. I only had £4 pay in my pocket, because the army still took the 2s/6d barrack-room robbery in advance, even though nobody would be in the barracks so how could there possibly be any bloody damage done to it? Another army squaddie-scam. Being back home for a bit was a welcome change from the marching and boot-shining and brass-button-polishing and whitening the webbing and more square-bashing. Even being back footing-digging and bricklaying and plate-fixing and listening to my father laying down the law and my older brothers bellowing at the younger ones – for a while.

When I got back to Kempston Barracks after the four weeks' leave, I was transferred to the Northamptonshire Regiment. The Northamptonshires were known as the 'Steelbacks' – some say because of all the steel mills around Northampton and Corby and Wellingborough and the rest of them spark-flying towns, while others say because of the men's reputation for taking a leathering from the lash without as much as a murmur. I liked the fact that it was a rum sporting regiment as well – for football and cricket and rugby and boxing and running. Every Wednesday afternoon, everyone had to go on a cross-country canter. The first run was four miles and a mile was added to each weekly run after that, until the maximum nine miles was reached. If you didn't do the run in the designated time, you had to do it over again the following Saturday afternoon; and again and again until you beat the time. Which was alright for the skinny long-legs but not too good for the heavier hang-behinds.

I wasn't long with the Northamptonshires before they sent me over to Austria.

Me on the left and mate Harry Church in
the Northampton Regiment.

6

Having a Few Laughs
with Pogs and BAFs

I was posted to Klagenfurt, in the region of the Austrian Alps known as Carinthia. It was in the southern part of the country, close to the borders of Italy and what used to be Yugoslavia back then, but is now Slovenia. There was tension in the region after the war, with Austria and Yugoslavia both claiming it as theirs. So the BTA, or British Troops in Austria, which was the nice new name they gave to the section of the Eighth Army the Northamptonshires were attached to, set up their headquarters in Klagenfurt, the capital of Carinthia – and Carinthia and neighbouring Styria formed the British occupation zone in liberated Austria until 1955.

We were sent there for eight weeks of intensive training and transported down to Harwich in lorries, then ferried over to the Hook of Holland. We travelled by train through the Low Countries and France and West Germany for a day and a half and I can remember the state Europe was in – even seven years after the war had ended. Especially Germany. The towns we passed through were a kind of charcoal grey – bombed out and blitzed out and burned out and begging. Pleading. Hands and knees through the half-streets and buildings with no roofs on them and people half-living in the rubble. Cologne was the worst. There was scorched and skin-burned evidence of the firestorm that happened on that night in 1942, when over a thousand bombers rained over two thousand tons of bombs down on the city. The pathetic children with degraded mothers – those who had mothers to be degraded – and the starving pensioners and the absence of domestic animals. It haunted my head and made me feel ashamed that anyone could have done this in the name of freedom and fair play. The devastation and level of destruction was unimaginable and I could only weep at the thought of what it was like for the people of that city when hell itself rained down from the skies on them. I know we'd been bombed – London and Liverpool and lots of other places in England – and the Nazis had done all kinds of devilish things in the name of normality. But nobody deserved that kind of retribution, that level of vindictiveness – especially the civilians who had no hand in the hellraising. I reckoned back then, going through the soot-sick and ash-blown towns, that the Allies should've spent a few more dollars helping them people to build the place back up and not leave it like it was for eighteen-year-olds like me and my mates to pass through and see and feel so ashamed.

The journey took us out of Germany after living and

sleeping on the fart-filled train for forty hours straight and we were finally in Austria. But I soon wished I was back on the flat lowlands and not up in the steep mountains. We disembarked at Klagenfurt and I thought we'd finally reached our destination. But we hadn't! We were put into three-ton lorries and driven six miles up the stomach-churning side of the Alps to a little place called Schmeltz. It was one of the steepest rides I'd ever been on – sheer and winding tracks with thousand-foot drops on my side of the lorry and me holding on to the man next to me, in case I fell out. And if the lorry went over, then it wouldn't have mattered who I was holding on to, I could've kissed my scut-end goodbye.

The place was a ski resort in wintertime and we were all under canvas in the hills and forests around it. It was part of the Brenner Pass, which they said was the location of the last big battle between the Russians and Germans at the end of World War Two and formed one of the 'ratlines', which was the system of escape routes for Nazis getting out of Europe after Germany was defeated. The ratlines were the first stage of the network that led to South America and the United States for wanted war criminals. Our ratline near Schmeltz was later made famous in the book *The Odessa Files* – ODESSA stood for Organisation Der Ehemaligen SS-Angehörigen, or the Organisation of Former SS-Members. See, you learn something new every educational day!

To me, living alfresco out in the woods was like a home away from home. I was well used to roughing it from all the times I ran away from the reform schools down the railway tracks with Lilly. Some of the city boys took a while to get used to it and we had a lot of them – from London and Liverpool and Birmingham and Bradford and all over. They had no idea how to look after themselves out in the bare backwoods conditions, but they soon learned. We all mucked in together and us country bumpkins showed 'em the ropes and there was no animosity or rivalry between the townies and the tony-lumpkins. We were all in it together, as the politicians say while they snigger up their sleeves nowadays. The other thing was the altitude; it bothered some people but never had any effect on me – at least, not until they made us march over the Alps.

Then it did!

But things were a lot more relaxed in cloud-level Schmeltz than they were back at the basic training barracks in Kempston. We were allowed to use the bars in the ski lodge on the weekends, if we weren't on duty – from Friday till Sunday. We paid our Austrian hosts with cigarettes instead of money – John Players and Woodbines and Weights and Senior Service and Churchills and State Express 777s. Two hundred fags would pay for a whole weekend's beer and food as well, and the crafty Austrians sold them on and made a fair old profit for themselves on the black market. It was better for us than paying with money. You see, we got paid in BAFs and 'Pogs' – British Armed Forces banknotes and small change tokens – and the bars wouldn't take the BAFs and the army cheated us on the exchange rate to local currency. At the time, we could've got sixteen marks for a pound sterling. But, of course, we didn't have pounds sterling, did we, we had bloody BAFs and the quartermaster only gave us fourteen marks for one BAF, which was supposed to be the equal of a pound sterling. But it wasn't and we lost two marks on every BAF we changed up. Another soldier stealth-tax! I'm telling you, the British Army could teach any Tory Chancellor of the Exchequer a thing or two about thievery.

We got fifty free cigarettes each week and we bought the rest with our BAFs – it was only one shilling for a pack of twenty – we smoked as much as we needed and then spent the surplus on beer in the ski-resort bar.

The NAAFI itself was in a tent and so was the cookhouse and everything else. A three-tonner would drive up from Klagenfurt once a day with provisions and we'd line up for whatever we wanted. It was fairly free and easy, like I said – there were no walls nor fences nor railings to hem us in and we could wander round the free-range tents on the mountainside and imagine we were yodelling a love song with Hedy Lamarr. All the cooking was done over open fires too, as there was no electricity nor gas nor nothing like that. We made our own ovens out of tin cans and made fire pits in the ground with stones that got red hot, and we could bake bread and roast meat and even dry our boots and socks after the rain had belted down, as it sometimes did out of the summertime sky.

We washed and shaved in cold water the whole time we were there and the Pioneer Company dug out trenches for us to use as latrines. The trenches were eighteen foot long by four foot wide and six foot deep, with a plank of wood running across the middle of them and sacking set up round them for privacy. It was easy enough to piss off the plank, but taking a dump was much more difficult and it was a definite advantage if you were an acrobat in civvy street. You had to squat down with trousers and cellular drawers round your ankles, and get your arsehole out over the edge of the plank because if you shat on the wood you got a bollocking and had to clean it and were told to make sure you hung your arse further out next time. That made some of the boys nervous and they'd squat out too far and, if they fell in – well, it all depended on what level the trench was filled to.

One trench was supposed to last a company of one hundred men for four weeks. The Pioneers were able, with a ratio of how much food we were given to eat and what percentage of that food turned into excrement, to work out how much shit it took to fill each trench. But now and then they got their capacities wrong, especially when most of the men would be down at the ski lodge stuffing their faces and drinking gallons of beer, and the latrines sometimes overflowed. In hot weather, they were full of maggots and stank to high heaven and that was the worst time to slip off the plank. The army probably looked on it as extra-curricular training, so we'd be able to keep our balance if ever something exploded close enough to perforate our eardrums. When the slurry was close to ground-level or beyond, the Pioneers dumped this chemical stuff in that killed everything, including the stink – but it had a peculiarly powerful pong of its own that hung like a toxic mist over the whole camp and I don't know which was worse, the smell of the shit or the smell of the industrial 'sanilav'. Once the chemicals had done their job, the Pioneers backfilled the trenches and that was that. If you work it out, with two trenches to each company for the duration of the eight weeks, the battalion left eighty latrines full of 432 cubic feet of good old British dung on the pristine Alpine environment, and that was just during the short time I was there.

There was no other entertainment of any kind in Schmeltz, apart from the ski lodge boozer, so we stayed in the bar from Friday till Sunday and slept where we sat. We took 200 cigarettes for beer and another 200 to smoke or play cards with. There was nothing else to do, except play bar skittles with the chain and ball. The barmaids weren't interested in us, they were making enough money from the cigarettes without dropping their drawers for soldier boys and there were very few other civilians on the mountain. We'd sleep heads bent down on the bar tables for a few hours when we'd had enough, then wake up and carry on drinking. The beer was Austrian 'normal' lager and, once, I fell asleep in a pool of it and when I woke up again I was stuck to the table-surface and had to be prised free. It was like I'd grown a new skin while I was forty-winking that was part me and part table, and I had to peel it off. It lay there on the floor with some of my old skin and most of the table varnish and I would have shot it if I'd had my 303 with me. God knows what the stuff was doing inside our stomachs. But there was nothing else to drink that had alcohol in it – except for schnapps and I never was a one for spirits, so I had to keep drinking the stuff all the time I was up on the mountain. After a weekend of boozing on the elastic beer, we'd make our way back to camp and fall into the tents for a few hours until Monday morning reveille and the duty-corporal screaming:

'Hands off cocks and on socks!'

And a new week would begin.

There was a full battalion of a thousand men on the mountain, split into ten companies of one hundred in each. I was in C Company. It was mostly full-time soldiers out there and only about 30 per-cent National Service boys like me. This was another money-saving scheme by the army: they had to pay their regulars £3/10s a week, but they only had to pay us eighteen-year-olds £1/2s/6d for the same work – less than half the cost of a regular recruit. Like I said, the British Army was always well up on ways to save money and could mind mice at a crossroads.[7] Us cheap-labour conscripts got all the donkey-work jobs as well – cleaning up the campsite and cookhouse duties and stag,[8] while the officers and NCOs and long-tour-of-duty wallahs went fishing. Unless, of course, you won the 'stick man's prize' for the best-presented soldier. If you could manage that, you got an easy life. I never won it, all the time I was in the army. I tried hard, mind you, but never ever got to be the best turned out. Even so, I wasn't as bad as Ralph Goodenough – Ralph couldn't iron because he was a clumsy clod and the rest of us would help him with it and also with polishing his shoes and applying his blanco. The sergeant would shout at him on parade, 'Goodenough, you're not bloody good enough!'

I used to put lengths of motorbike chain in the turn-ups of my trousers to make 'em hang better. But the sergeant major would come round and tap the trouser legs with his stick and, if they

7 i.e. very crafty.
8 Guard duty.

clanked, you went on three days' jankers. You'd have to paint the coal white and then the sergeant major would come round and shout, 'What's that coal doing white? It should be black!'

Then you'd have to paint it black again.

Once you got three days' jankers, time and again it turned into seven days for some reason. The NCOs picked on the janker-wallahs, and there was no pleasing the buggers. They'd have it right in for you and you'd be put on a 'fizzer' for no flippin' reason, which is what they called a 252. The least little thing and you'd find yourself having to fizz up to the captain's office and get another three or four days. Luckily for me, except for the motor-bike chains, I kept my nose clean while I was up the mountain in Schmeltz and, unlike Kempston Barracks in Bedford, I didn't have to do much jankers the whole time I was there.

The most boring thing was guard duty – or stag as we called it – because there was nothing for us to guard against. The Germans were gone, except for the ones trying to sneak out of Europe through the ratlines – and I never saw none of them. And the Yugoslavs had given up their claim to the region. So, there wasn't much to mind. We had to do twelve-hour and twenty-four-hour stints of stag. The twelve-hour stint was two hours on and two hours off and you were supposed to get some kip when you were off. But you'd be just getting into a nice dainty dream with Deborah Kerr when you'd be woken up again. The twenty-four-hour stint was a bit better, because it was two hours on and four hours off, so at least you got a bit more time in the bunk with Betty Grable. But the good thing was, only one parade a day, in the morning if you were on day duty or in the evening on the night shift. Otherwise it was alright and I didn't mind being up there in the high Böhmerwald at all. Certainly better than square-bashing in Bedford.

One weekend, as I was making my way down to the ski resort for a few days' drinking of the polyurethane Pilsner, I came across this sergeant fishing in a small stream with a piece of string and a hook attached to a stick. He called me over and pointed to the ground. So, not wanting to disobey a direct order, I sat down beside him and asked if he'd caught anything.

'Not biting today.'

'Why's that?'

'I suppose . . . they ain't hungry.'

The man had ginger hair and a ginger moustache and he looked real fearsome to a young lad like me. But, in reality, he was as nice as ninepence. He told me his name was Bill Kelly and he was about thirty-five years old and that was fairly ancient to me – nearly as old as my father. You could tell he'd seen a thing or two in his life and I was brought up to respect people who'd seen more than I had. Don't forget, there weren't any teenagers in those days. Even though I was only eighteen, I was a man in the eyes of my elders and expected to behave like a man and not like a bothersome boy. And proper men had respect for those who'd been around and seen more than them. Bill told me he'd joined the army when he was in his twenties, on a 22-year tour – and he still had a few years left to go. He'd served in the Gloucestershire Regiment during the war and he had also served in Korea, a war that started in 1950 that nobody knew much about nor wanted to and was still going on. He'd been made up to King's Sergeant for bravery in battle out there in the Far East and this was a rare honour, only given for great acts of carnage or courage. He never said what he did in Korea, but he was in the Glorious Gloucesters with a lot of other heroes who were decorated for bravery out there, and maybe that's where old Bill Kelly got his medal too, at Imjin River. It wouldn't have surprised me – back to back with the rest of the Gloucesters, shooting from the hip and sprouting arrows.

I found out afterwards that the battle took place during the Chinese Spring Offensive in April 1951, when the little devils were trying to recapture Seoul, which was taken in an earlier offensive by the Americans. The British 29th Infantry Brigade was positioned on the Imjin River and included the Gloucestershire Regiment. The British soldiers were a mixture of regulars like Bill Kelly and reservists and National Service boys like me, and they were supported by light artillery and dumb blondes[9] and battering rams. The 29th Brigade, with its four battalions, had to cover a twelve-mile front, and there wasn't a cat's chance in a dog-pound of forming a continuous line. So the men were spread out in separate little unit positions, with the Gloucesters guarding a ford over the Imjin, known as Gloucester Crossing. The scattered deployment weakened the defence of the front, along with the lack of heavy artillery and any sign of intelligence on the part of the officers. No other defensive plans nor preparations were made, because the British didn't expect to have to hold the position for more than the time it takes to make

9 Artillery officers.

thirty cups of tea. But, during the night of 22 April 1951, the Gloucesters had to fight fiercely with Chinese units trying to cross the river and, by the next morning, they'd suffered severe casualties.

Next day, American and Belgian forces were retreating and taking up new positions south of the Gloucesters, who were still holding, despite their heavy losses. A, C and D Companies were eventually withdrawn to Hill 235, which became known as Gloucester Hill, but B Company wasn't able to get back because they were pinned down by the Chinese. They say B Company drove back seven Chinese assaults before they were finally able to withdraw to Hill 235, but only seventeen men were still alive. And they weren't out of the woods yet – because of the Chinese deep penetration of the line, between the Gloucesters and the rest of the defending armies, the Gloucesters were cut off. M-24 and Centurion tanks were sent to relieve them but, would you believe this, the lead tank was hit by Chinese fire and knocked out and blocked the bloody route. Further progress towards the Gloucesters was impossible, according to the American Brigade Commander, so he withdrew the relief force and left the Gloucesters to it on their own. No further attempts to relieve them were made because, on 25 April, the order was issued for all forces to withdraw to a new defensive position, further south.

The Gloucesters' situation on Hill 235 made it impossible for them to join the retreat. B and C companies suffered such heavy losses that they had to be merged into one company, and even attempts to supply them by air failed, due to heavy Chinese fire. Despite their heavy casualties, the Gloucesters held their position

on Hill 235, even after they lost their artillery support on 25 April.
But they couldn't hold out for ever. The brigadier in charge had
to make a decision, try to break out or surrender. He decided they
ought to make a break for it and try to get back to the British lines
as best they could. It was every man for himself. Only the
remains of D Company escaped successfully from Gloucester
Hill and finally reached the safety of friendly lines after several
days' fighting a running rearguard action. The rest of the battalion was either killed or taken prisoner.

I was sure this was what Bill Kelly got his King's Sergeant
stripes for. But Bill didn't want to talk about it and he didn't want
to be a sergeant neither. He had no truck with officers, NCOs or
otherwise, and he couldn't bring himself to give orders to anybody. He didn't want responsibility – especially in Korea, because
he saw what happens when you put idiots in charge of men's
lives. Not that he was an idiot or anything, and he'd probably
have been better than half the officers in the entire British and
American armies – but he just didn't have the stomach for it. He
just wanted to be a private soldier and the whole thing made him
go a bit doolally. As a King's Sergeant, Bill couldn't lose his
stripes unless he was court-martialled.

Old Bill played on this and seldom did any normal duty. He
told me he was trying to work his ticket and make them take back
the stripes – he hated being a sergeant and wanted the buggers to
tell him what to do and not have to be the one to do the telling.
I asked him why he took the rank in the first place and he told me
he had no choice. You can't refuse a King's Sergeant promotion
when you get made up in battle. He didn't know he was being put

forward and when the stripes came through from the King, he wasn't allowed to turn them down. But Bill was just an ordinary soldier and he didn't like the larrikins in the sergeants' mess. So he did everything in his power to get back to where he was before he became a hero – to no avail. The army wouldn't demote him because it would've been a disgrace to the regiment to knock down a King's Sergeant. He'd go AWOL for a month at a time and nobody'd know where he was, then he'd just come strolling back into camp when he was ready. I once saw him sitting in the middle of the parade ground with a bucket of water and a line and hook, fishing – just to defy them. But they all just ignored him, from the colonels down to the corporals. He would've had to commit murder to get himself court-martialled and, even then, they probably would have let him off. There was no way he could lose his stripes, no matter what he did.

Bill asked where I was going and I told him I was going down to the bar at the ski lodge for a drink or two.

'How much money you got?'

'Four hundred fags.'

'That should do the two of us.'

When we got into the bar, the Austrians running it frowned at Bill and asked him if he was going to make trouble.

'Only if I don't get served.'

But he didn't make any trouble that weekend and we had a great session on the skin-graft lager and I enjoyed getting to know 'Mad Bill', as he was generally known. He took a shine to me too, for some reason, and we often got drunk together after that – thirty-six hours on the lash at a time, singing all the Frankie

Laine and Johnnie Ray songs. There could be forty or fifty men in that bar at any one time and Bill Kelly never had to buy himself a drink, that's how much respect he got from the other soldiers, despite never talking about what he did in Korea or how he came to be a hero.

We continued our training doing night schemes, or manoeuvres, as they're called now, with one company defending a position and another company attacking it. We'd come across broken-up tanks from the last big battle of World War Two — Russian and German and American — but not much else to take home as souvenirs. All the rest of the small arms and ordnance had been half-inched by the time we got there. Because I had a reputation for being a bit of a sharpshooter, they put me on a Browning water-cooled heavy-machine-gun. It took five men to operate this beast and we had to set it up on a tripod and aim it at a tree that was about three-quarters of a mile away, down the valley. The gun needed three five-gallon jerry cans of water to keep it cool, and three spare barrels, because they got red hot if they weren't rotated and topped up with the water. We were told to fire the gun at the tree down the valley all night long, until we used up all the ammunition.

The Browning was a good old gun and very accurate, but it took till Christmas to set up and too many men to operate, so it was at the end of its days. The 303 bullets used in the gun were on a long belt and every third bullet was a tracer, so you could see if you were on target at night. We started firing the gun at 1900 hours that night and didn't stop till 0500 hours the next morning, doing two hours on and two hours off between the five of us. We must've used up 20,000 rounds of ammunition and ruined the four water-cooled barrels. The tree we were aiming at was at least eight foot in diameter and by morning it was completely cut down and on fire from the tracers. The gun was then broken down and buried, along with whatever ammo was left. The old Browning was obsolete and was being replaced by the LMG and they didn't want to have to lug it with us.

Because they'd decided to make us march over the Alps to toughen us up.

7

It's a Pest to Lose Your
Cherry in Trieste

They told us it would be an easy little 125-mile trek on foot over the mountains and down into Trieste in Northern Italy – a walk in the Alpine Park. By 0600 hours on the morning when we finished shooting the shit out of the forest with the Browning, we'd cleaned up all our equipment and were ready for breakfast. After the grub, we began packing up all our gear and getting ready to march up over the top of the three-headed mountains and down the other side. All our kitbags were loaded onto lorries and driven down to Klagenfurt railway station to take the easy route by train to Trieste. But we had to walk, carrying our big packs and small packs and ammunition pouches and weapons, along with three of each item of uniform – shirts and socks and shorts and all our cleaning gear. Every night after making camp, we had to wash and dry and iron all the clothes we'd used during the day – all that after

marching twenty-five miles over terrain that would've intimi-
dated an ibex.

We set off at 0930 hours, the whole battalion, and we marched
for the first hour to the sound of the regimental band playing all
the old touring tunes, like 'It's a Long Way to Tipperary' and
'Pack up Your Troubles in Your Old Kit Bag' and that sort of
schmozzle. And we all sang along with the band to cheer our cold
hearts up. We marched for fifty minutes in every hour and then
had a ten-minute breather before setting off again, and we had a
half-hour break from 1230 hours to 1300 hours for a midday meal
and a cuppa java. We made camp under canvas each night, always
a fair distance away from the nearest village, because the officers
knew we'd be too knackered for trekking a few extra miles to
gatecrash a Bierkeller or interfere with some Fraulein. And they
were right.

By the end of the first day, most of us were suffering from
sore feet and blisters. We pricked the blisters and then soaked our
feet in cold salted water for an hour. We were told not to use
bandages or plasters, because these would crease up when we
marched again and cause more damage than they cured. We also
carried what they called 'poncho' waterproofs. These were
bivouac sacks and they had to be set up every night with two
sticks, one at each end and the 'poncho' draped over the top. It
stood about two-and-a-half foot off the ground and we had to
crawl in like crabs to sleep, with no ground sheet or nothing, so
if it rained we got wet to the winkles. The slightly good thing
about it was we were on released duties, which meant no blancoing and barrack-room bullshite like that. Apart from being

expected to keep as clean as we could, it was battleground conditions.

Going up to the top of the mountains was hard. The altitude got to all of us, including me. I mean, we were going up 8,000 feet from a position that was already 3,000 feet above sea level. We made the last half-mile almost crawling on our hands and knees and gasping for a gobful of breath. And going down the other side was as bad as going up. Sheer as a nylon on the top of a thigh and we were slipping and sliding and knocking each other over and losing our kit and rifles and it was chaos – until it levelled out a bit down in the foothills on the Italian side and we could march properly and not like a bunch of rubber-legged Max Walls.

It took five days and nights to get down to the Karst Plateau and, on the last day, we were picked up at 1400 hours by three-ton lorries about ten miles out and driven the rest of the route to the outskirts of Trieste. We then had to get out of the vehicles and form up and march the remaining mile or so through the streets of the old *fin-de-siècle* city to the sound of the regimental band playing 'The British Grenadiers'. We strutted in with bayonets fixed to let the locals know we'd arrived and were ready for any kind of rowdiness. The Brits were running the show and we weren't going to take any nonsense from no half-baked liberationist. Trieste housed the biggest ammunitions dump in the world at the time and it was going to be our job to look after it. But the Italians hated us – they loved the Yanks, but hated us British – don't ask me why, I could never figure that one out – maybe because of the Mafioso. There was no welcoming reception, just scowls from the partisans passing along the streets – but we took no notice.

You may be asking yourself what we were doing there in the first place. Well, it was like this – on 30 April 1945, the Italian anti-fascists started a riot against the German occupiers. The next day, the Yugoslav partisans arrived in support and managed to take over most of the city, except for the castle of San Giusto, where the Germans held out for another day until they finally surrendered to the 2nd New Zealand Division of the Allied Forces, who straight away turned them over to the Yugoslavs. After that, the Yugoslavs held full control of the city and hundreds of local Italian nationalists and anti-communists and fascists and Nazi collaborators 'disappeared'. Most of them were murdered and thrown into potholes on the Karst Plateau and the rest sent to Yugoslav concentration camps. The period of occupation was known to the Italians as 'the forty days of Trieste' and it came to an end in June 1945 when an agreement was reached between the Yugoslav leader Tito and Britain's Field Marshall Alexander. The Yugoslavs withdrew from Trieste, which came under joint British and US military administration. In 1947, Trieste was declared an independent city state under the protection of the United Nations and divided into two zones, A and B. The A zone was governed by the Yanks and the British – our lot was called BETFOR, British Element Trieste Forces. The B zone was controlled by the Yugoslav People's Army. This lasted up till 1954, when A zone became part of Italy and B zone became part of Yugoslavia. In 1952, when I was there, the Yugoslavs still reckoned the whole shebang belonged to them and we had to make sure they stayed where they belonged.

Another thing the generals were worried about was the fact, like I just said, that the largest ammunitions dump in the entire world was situated in Trieste, and it was our job to guard it. If anything went awry and it happened to explode for any reason, half of Europe would've gone up with it. So now you know what all the fuss and fidgeting was about. Anyway, we marched the one-and-a-half miles from where the lorries dropped us off to the barracks where we were to be stationed. The place wasn't much, mind you, similar I suppose to the barracks in Bedford where I'd done my basic training, and as soon as we got there the duty sergeant gave us a lecture about steering clear of the wine and the women whenever we went into town. This was because you got put on a charge if you caught any venereal disease and you lost wages until you were cured – and the local vino was considered too strong for our delicate English digestive systems. None of us took any notice of him, of course, and we all looked forward to getting out and getting absolutely plastered and pestering the indigenous *donne*.

As soon as we got the chance, three of us decided to take the plunge and go on the town. The sergeant asked for our regimental numbers in case we got captured by the enemy and they had to have a body count or something, and I gave him John Wells's number – if you remember, he was one of the lads from Treacle Bumstead who I joined up with. We booked out at the guardroom and off we went. I did this in case I got into any trouble, which was quite likely for me. If that happened, John would get pulled for it. I'd just have to climb over the fence and be back in camp by the morning. Nasty, I know. But he'd have done the same for me and I'm sure he did – many times. It was a trick I used all the time and got away with it too – until the redcaps got to know me.

Anyway, we headed off to Gonorrhoea Park, as the centre of town was euphemistically called, but we couldn't afford a prozzie on our army pay – the girls were charging 200 lira, which was about ten bob in those days, and that was half our weekly wages of one pound sterling. So we went into this bar, which was rather a rough old dive – full of squaddies and stag-dodgers and signalmen and no locals, except for the bar staff. We ordered three drinks, thinking we'd be served three glasses of wine like in a civilised establishment. But, instead, we were served three litre bottles. It cost about 1s/6d a bottle and it was hairy old rotgut, with toenails and everything floating about in it. Now, I'd never drunk wine before and I was downing it like beer and each of us bought a round apiece – so that was three litres each and we drunk them all in about an hour.

We were stocious drunk by then, but we didn't know it, so we decided to go to a different bar. Well, as soon as we hit the air outside, we went all rubber-legged like Max Wall again and thought we were coming déjà-vu down the Alps, but we were only on the pavement. Then we fell down like three sacks of potatoes. It was like being hit on the back of the head with a four-pound lump hammer and it wasn't long before we were dragged back to our feet by the redcaps. Now, they could've banged us up in their cells overnight and, when we got back to barracks next morning, we'd be on a charge for going AWOL. But this night they must've been on the happy pills or else they didn't want to have to put up with us all night long, sicking and shouting, because they took us back to our own guardhouse. Like an idiot, I forgot I checked out with John Wells's number and I gave my own on the stumble-bumble way back in.

'You're not in the book, Sears.'

'There wash no one here when I left, Corporal.'

'The guardhouse is never left empty, Sears.'

'Then how come there wash no one here?'

They gave up trying to get any sense out of me and threw the three of us into the cells. Reveille was at 0600 hours and my head was banging like a mallet-bell on a blacksmith's anvil. I struggled over to the cookhouse for a bit of breakfast but, as soon as I swallowed a cup of tea, I was back being as drunk as I was the night before and falling fruit-faced all over the place. Back into the cells! This went on for the next two days – as soon as I took a cup of tea or cocoa or water, I was back drunk again. So I was left languishing in the flowery dell until I finally sobered up on the third day.

When at last I could stand up straight, I was put on CO's Orders and got seven days' jankers. This meant reporting to the duty officer in the guardhouse every morning at 0800 hours and being given the shittiest jobs going. Mine was to weed an acre of Scotch thistle they'd brought over specially and planted just for the purpose of teaching me a lesson. I had to get each thistle up without damaging the roots and carefully place it into a box full of soil. When they were all up, I had to replant them again that same evening, before the Adriatic air damaged their delicate

Highland cell structure. They never gave me no gloves or nothing and the prickly old thistles tore at my hands, even though they were hardened from the building sites. My two partners in crime had to dust off this big pile of coal and paint it pure white. Next day, I had to paint it back black again – and this is how it went on for the full seven days. It was hot in Trieste and they didn't need the coal for anything else but to punish people who got out of line. In the end, we painted one side of the coal lumps white and the other side black and then all we had to do was turn it over and get rid of the paint down the drains.

This ammunitions dump I told you about earlier was situated in the Montebello area of Trieste. It covered about five square miles and had an outer perimeter fence and an inner perimeter fence, with high guard towers at all four corners. The towers were about thirty foot high and in close communication with each other and to the main guardhouse by field phone. It was like a little town in itself and it had a trotting track round it. There was every type of ammunition you could think of stored there, all left over from World War Two. It was kept in that particular place because Trieste was fairly central for all the other flashpoint areas at the time – like Cyprus and the Middle East and North Africa and East Germany. It was 48-hour guard duty at a time and it got as boring as Ballylookbackwards in a blizzard. I mean, all the time I was there I only saw one person close to the perimeter. And even then I had to ring up the second lieutenant and ask for permission to fire.

'Is he inside the perimeter or outside?'

'Not sure, sir . . . maybe between the fences, sir.'

'Fire at him, Sears, but don't hit him.'

'Why not, sir?'

'He could be anybody. We don't want an international incident.'

I fired and whoever it was turned round and ran away. They sent out a search party, but never found no sign of the snooper.

Apart from that, nothing much ever happened, so on my watch I used to organise singing competitions over the field phone – everyone would be marked on a scale of one to ten and the winner got a hundred cigarettes. We'd sing all the latest stuff we heard on the radio, like 'In the Cool, Cool, Cool of the Evening' and 'Don't Let the Stars Get in Your Eyes' and 'Walkin' My Baby Back Home' and 'To Know You (Is to Love You)' and 'Hey Good Lookin'' and all the other hits of the early 1950s. Everybody won sooner or later – everybody got their fifteen minutes of fame and won the fags and the officers turned a blind eye to it all. I suppose they reckoned it was good for morale – 'Sears' singsong' – and it was!

The next on my list of things to do was lose my virginity. I was eighteen and still had hold of my cherry and, while this wasn't unusual in them days, unlike today, in the army it was getting to be a source of embarrassment for me – what with all the others bragging about sorts and strumpets and strippers and slappers and streetwalkers. So, the cherry had to go. Anyway, I decided to hell with the expense, I was going to get myself a lady of the night and do the deed once and for all. So I set off for Gonorrhoea Park with the lira clutched in my sweaty fist and a packet of French letters in my pocket.

After mooching about for a while, looking like a lost dog, I saw this girl and got up enough courage to approach her.

'How much?'

'Two hundred lira.'

'OK.'

She told me to follow her, but to stay a few yards behind, just in case the redcaps were watching. It was more than likely she was Yugoslavian, as most of the prostitutes were, and if the British MPs caught her, she'd be handed over to battalion police and sent back to Yugoslavia and God only knew what would've happened to her then. She was older than me – maybe twenty-five or so – and she looked like a film star, with her olive skin and brunette hair and red lips and flashing eyes. I followed her until we came to a quiet spot at the back of the British Military Hospital, which had a high wire fence round it.

'Lira.'

'OK . . . here.'

I gave her the money in advance of gratification and she lay down on the grass. I dropped my strides and started fiddling with the French letter and she was waiting patiently for me to get myself sorted. The next thing, this big Alsatian dog came bounding up on the other side of the fence, barking and behaving like a flea-infested lunatic, and the girl jumped up and took out to run and I tried to do the same, only my trousers were down round my ankles and the French letter stretched over my dick and index finger and I fell over five times before I managed to pull the strides back up. By this time the girl was long gone – and so was my lump of lira. When I got back to camp, all my mates were asking what was it like, Ken, and I said it was great. I never saw that girl again.

During my stay in Trieste, a big battle manoeuvre was organised between the British and American forces, with the Yanks defending the high ground and us attacking from below. The Americans were all gunned up with steel helmets and automatics and us with our berets and 303s. I said to myself, 'Sod this for a game of soldiers!'

But the alternative to taking part was cookhouse duties, so it was the easiest of two evils. Everyone was issued with a couple of armbands – one red and one blue – and we were to put these on if a referee decided we'd been shot, the blue armband for a wound and the red for a kill. I got killed on the second day and I knew this meant back to the field kitchen to stir the stewpots. So, when nobody was looking, I took the red armband off and made my way back to my lines and nary a one was the wiser. But the officer wanted to know why I was an hour behind everyone else.

'Where you been, Sears?'

'Had to take a shit, sir.'

'A long shit, Sears.'

'Couldn't find a private spot, sir.'

'Get back in line!'

The next thing I knew was this other referee sticks his wooden head up.

'That man there, you're wounded.'

'What man where?'

'That man.'

'You, Sears.'

'What? I'm already dead.'

'Where's your red armband?'

What a bugger. I just got back when I'm shot again and this time I had no get-out as the Rupert[10] was right beside me when it happened. So, blue armband on and traipse off to the field kitchen for the next five days.

When the manoeuvre was over, we heard that one of our lads had been hit on the side of the head by a two-inch smoke-mortar bomb and was in a critical condition on account of a substantial chunk having been taken out of his brain. Only blank rounds were supposed to be used – mock battle, mock bullets – but the stupid Yanks were pissing about as usual and firing smoke bombs just for the fun of it and it ended in tears for our lad. An enquiry was held and the Americans denied all knowledge and the British High Command hushed it up. The young eighteen-year-old soldier was flown back to a military hospital in England and none of us ever heard anything about him again. But we all knew it was a cover-up, with top officers involved and all kissing Uncle Sam's American arse.

The other manoeuvres we used to have to do in Trieste were called 'boat-landing schemes', where we'd practise mock offensive landings. We'd have to take the 'boats' – as we called them but they were really landing craft – out and try to land assault troops at designated points along the coast. But the Adriatic

10 Officer.

currents would sometimes take us up into the Yugoslav zone and the crucchi cockwaggers would open fire on us with live ammo. We only had blanks in our Lee-Enfields and there'd be men scrambling and screaming everywhere, falling over each other to get back into the boats and the Yugos laughing their heads off and gesturing with their genitals. Nobody ever got hit, to my knowledge, anyways, but we never hung around too long to test their aim.

I marched into Trieste with my regiment in July 1952, and marched out again in September, three months later. But before I went, I got another opportunity to lose my virginity. I had this job in the stores and was detailed to do the grocery delivery to the married quarters in a 15cwt lorry with another private called Nunley, also from the Steelbacks. What Nunley didn't tell me was that he was shagging the RSM's wife, Mrs Smart, and one delivery I went to her quarters instead of him. This must've been an oversight on his part, or maybe he was getting tired of her and wanted me to take over his duties. If he was, he should've mentioned it. Anyway, I went in and she offered me a cuppa, which would've been unfriendly of me to turn down and she might say something to her high-stepping husband and get me put on a fizzer. So I sat down. The next thing, she was sitting on top of me and she was a big woman of forty and I was a skinny eighteen-year-old and I spilt the tea into my lap trying to get out from under her. Ignorant of the opposite sex as I was, I still knew she was propositioning me and I also knew I was in trouble – either way. I mean, if I moved on her and the RSM found out, he'd have my ears for ashtrays – but if I didn't move on her, she'd be a woman scorned and I'd be on the butt-end of the fury from hell. Much as I wanted to lose my helmet-head, the thought of the RSM's purple puss put a damper on any desire I might have had. So, I opted for the latter option and left the quarters sharpish, cursing Nunley into the ground and out of it.

Mrs Smart told her husband I had dirty potato-pickers' knees and I got seven days' jankers and lost my cushy job.

What an unbridled buggeration!

8

Finding God in the Black Forest

At the end of September, the Northamptonshire Regiment was transferred to Wuppertal in West Germany. The city was situated in the industrial heartland of the crippled country, with Dusseldorf to the west and Essen to the north, and so it was certainly a strategic place – even though half of it had been blown to bits by Allied bombing during World War Two. We travelled by train for two days, through northern Italy and back across the Alps into Austria – only this time we didn't have to walk. Then up through Germany into the Rhineland and Westphalia. On the first night, I was detailed to guard the carriage containing all the officers' personal luggage and the baggage belonging to their wives. My stag was from 2400 hours till 0200 hours and I was all alone in a dim-lit carriage that was about forty foot long and crammed with cases and crates and boxes and bags and trunks and treasure-chests. There were aisles between the luggage so the handlers could get up and down and find stuff if it was wanted urgently. I was told to keep the door locked and not to let no one in, unless they could identify themselves.

About 0100 hours, I heard this soft knocking on the carriage door. I was half asleep and dreaming I was awake, so I easily slipped back into my light slumber. Then it came again – 'knock, knock, knock' – three times.

'Who's there?'

'It's Mrs Whelan. Captain Whelan's wife.'

'Yes, ma'am, what can I do for you?'

'You can let me in.'

'What for?

'I need to get some clean glasses from my hospitality box.'

It seemed a reasonable enough request to me, they might be having drinks in their compartment and not want to mix the rum and the mother's ruin in the same glass. And I wasn't alert enough to wonder why she didn't send an orderly along for them. So I opened the door.

Mrs Whelan slipped quickly into the carriage, dressed only in a sheer see-through negligee, and I knew straight away it wasn't clean glasses she was after. Now let me say this, Mrs Whelan wasn't remotely like Mrs Smart – she was a very beautiful and sophisticated-looking lady in her thirties. Still a fair bit older than myself at the time, but to me she looked like every movie star I'd ever seen – five-foot-four and blonde and a figure you could time an egg with. She recognised me from the grocery delivery in Trieste and this was another dangerous situation. But I remembered what happened when I turned Mrs Smart down and a good horse is never a bad colour. I didn't get much time to think about it because she grabbed hold of me and we slipped down onto the floor between the panniers and the portmanteaux and this was it – my young years of innocence were about to end. We were kissing wildly and hands going everywhere and I forgot to lock the door and it was then I heard this gruff voice in the beguiling dim-light.

'Celia . . .'

We both stopped. Stock still. Silent.

'Celia . . .'

She stood up quickly and straightened her hair.

'Over here, George.'

It was Captain Whelan – come to find his wife or a clean glass. I got up quickly after her but there was a bulge in my trousers that I couldn't get rid of and I'm sure he saw it – dim light or no dim light.

'What's going on?'

'Nothing, George.'

'We're looking for Mrs Whelan's box, sir.'

'And have you found it?'

He knew what was going on and I'd live to regret this night once we got to Wuppertal. But it was something that happened all the time – officers pissed and ignoring their wives or belting them about and the women going elsewhere for either attention or revenge – or both. And it seemed like fate and provenance were both conspiring against me and I was never ever going to lose my cherry.

*

We arrived at Wuppertal station at 0900 hours and were told to bull all our kit up and be prepared to march from the station to our new barracks – two hours away – even though it was only about four miles, up a hill near the centre of town. The reason it took two hours to get there is because the regimental band lost their way and we marched over the same route several times. I knew this because I saw the overhead railway twice and it was the only one in the world at the time. Maybe they didn't get lost. Maybe the long march was deliberate. You never knew why the British Army ever did what it did – and you never asked neither. But it was all worth it when we got to the new barracks. These were former SS quarters and were like a panjandrum's palace compared to what we were used to. Four soldiers to each individual room – unheard of in any other theatre of the British Army. If even a light bulb blew, all you had to do was open a small box in the corridor and flick a switch. No more mending fuses in the dark – genius German technology that wouldn't arrive in England for another twenty years. Military dolce vita with all the amenities – private toilets and tallboys and cupboards to keep our gear in.

What more could any conscript want?

We settled into our new surroundings and, next day, after the usual 0800 hours parade, we were told we could have the day off – unless we had jankers to perform. I decided to go into Wuppertal and suss out the lay of the land. It was a Wednesday and I didn't have all that much money, so I steered clear of the brothels and the bad women and used the cigarette black market to earn a few marks. I did this wherever I went – Klagenfurt or

Wuppertal or Lunenburg, selling the fags in flop shops[11] and clubs for four or five times what I paid for 'em. I could get ten marks for a hundred ciggies, after paying only five shillings in the NAAFI. It was a good way of supplementing the pound a week the army paid us National Service boys and I took good advantage of it whenever I could. I decided to first suss out the local British Legion, where the beer was cheap and they sold good old English ale like Red Shield and White Shield, that was still fermenting in the bottom of the bottles and would blow your head off if you shook it up. They sold Charrington's draught bitter and mild too, and they didn't allow women in unless they had a membership card – and membership cards weren't given to women. But some of the more inventive recruits got away with smuggling a strumpet or two in when the commissionaire was looking the other way and feeling the texture of the five-mark note between his fingers. And, if it wasn't wrong – it must've been right.

After slouching round the British Legion, I checked out the NAAFI Hotel, where you could book a room by the hour but there was no drinking allowed. If it wasn't one thing, it was the other – always the way! So I didn't stay there long. It was supposed to be a place for soldiers to kip down if they were booked out for a long weekend. In fact, it was a cathouse wearing camouflage, once you'd had a good drink at an alternative venue first – and most certainly better than the perimeter fence round a military hospital. I made a mental note of that – for

11 Bawdy houses.

future reference. On from there into the German jazz clubs for a few lagers with the louts and a jive with the jukebox. The women there weren't prostitutes, they were just there for the dancing and you didn't try it on with them or you got belted across the boatrace. These places were hip and played all the latest hits and they could have a four-piece combo on stage and a singer and waiter service. I found I could drink all night and just sign a tab at the end of the session for the bill to be brought. Paradise Alley!

But life soon descended into the daily routine of parades and posturing and rifle ranges and guard duties, and old Captain Whelan remembered me from the dim-lit train carriage and found fault with everything I did. There was jankers for this and jankers for that and jankers on top of jankers from the bugger – even though he interrupted us before it got interesting with his wife and I felt like I was being punished for nothing. Although you could dodge the jankers if you could find someone else who was willing to do it for you – and for ten bob, which was half a week's wages. The other way of getting out of all duties and getting fed special grub was to join the boxing team – but it meant training all the time and getting belted round the head by blokes bigger than you. I took this option and finally got my own back when the season started. All the officers had to go in the ring and Whelan was in the same weight division as me and when I saw him in the opposite corner, I smiled on the inside of my face. Then I knocked seven shades of shite out of him and he tended to leave me alone after that.

But I needed more than the boxing to break the monotony of

barracks life and, a few weeks later, I saw a notice on the Battalion Orders of the Day:

An Invitation
to any soldier interested.
A ten-day course of Catholic Religious Instruction.
In the Black Forest.

Now, I'd had enough of the Catholics after what they did to me when I was running away from the NCHO reform school, but I'd heard a lot about the Black Forest region of Germany and I wanted to see it for myself. So I put my name forward. As well as that, they told me my wages would increase by an extra ten bob a week if I passed the course with flying colours, and I knew that would be a doddle after it'd been beaten into me back when I was eleven years old.

I was accepted for the course with five other likely lads and we all set off on a train south through Hessen and Baden-Wurttemberg to the Schwarzwald. After a time-flying journey of nearly thirty hours through the Grimm and goblin-filled Deutschland, we were taken the rest of the remote way in the back of a lorry and we passed through the most beautiful country I'd ever seen. I mean, I thought it was something up in the ski resort of Schmeltz, but this was the Garden of all Edens. And I'll say this, after the foreign exploits of my earlier life, I never really had a wish or a whistle to travel later on. But this is definitely one place I'd dearly love to see again – if it's still there. I can't explain in words the effect it had on me, feeling it in my soul for the first time. You can make sounds like 'magnificent' and 'majestic' and 'pretty' and 'picturesque', but they're just sounds without much real meaning when it comes to expressing how I felt that day, on first stepping into this fairytale place.

The retreat itself was like a miniature medieval castle, with a keep and towers and ramparts and merlons and parapets, and I thought I'd been taken back in time and half expected Sir Lancelot to come clip-clopping out in his shining armour and poniards and pennants. There was about a dozen nuns in this place and they came out smiling to greet us when we arrived. They wore black habits, with them white wide-brimmed hats, and some were young and some were old, but they were all angelic. Would you believe, I never knew the name of this place, nor the order of the nuns, but I'll never forget its wonderment – and I'll never understand how it survived the destruction of World War Two without a scratch or a blemish on its serene face.

Our sleeping quarters were as good as the SS billet back at Wuppertal. Two men to a room and we had a proper bed each and clean dry sheets every day. We were woken at 0700 hours on the first morning by a nun asking what we wanted for breakfast. We couldn't believe this at first and thought we were either dead or dreaming. But it was true. All the nuns spoke English with a strange accent and breakfast was egg and bacon and sausage and beans and tomatoes and pots of tea with toast and marmalade. We weren't dreaming, so we were sure we must've died during the night and, if this was Catholic heaven, they had me converted. After breakfast, we made our beds and cleaned our boots and went to class at 0930 hours. We were taken to a kind of schoolroom with desks and dusters and it brought back some bad old memories for me. But they didn't last long, because this place was entirely different from the first Catholic school I was abducted to. The lessons were all about the Bible and how the world began and I felt like a child again, only I wasn't being shouted at and belted and kicked for not knowing my catechism.

The main gist of the course seemed to be an explanation of the dogma of the Catholic Church, but in a gentle and tolerant way, not in a bullying, shouting, stick-swinging way. The nuns asked us questions in a soft tone of voice that suggested they thought we were some childlike people from back when time began – questions like what we knew about Christ (and I knew a lot about Him and most of it I didn't like). I had the answers the other lads didn't have, who were all Church of England and had never seen the inside of a confessional box. And for the first time I felt some little appreciation for the religious doctrine that had been bashed into me, back when I was a boy. I never could understand why the army sent us on that course. Nor do I know what they expected us to get from it. Maybe they were anticipating a serious shortage of chaplains in future conflicts or something. They never said and I never asked. They just wanted to know how we got on and if we passed the exam at the end – which we all did, thanks to my reform-school experiences. It didn't encourage me to fall in love with orthodox religion or to embrace the Catholic Church, but it gave me something –

something that's with me still. It gave me a sense of serenity that I feel at times when I think back – a sense that there is some wider thing, other than us mucky little mortals. Maybe it's not the heaven and hell that's preached to us from the pulpits – maybe it's not the gods or devils we're warned about. But there is something.

And I found it back there in the Black Forest – in among the trees.

If we thought the first morning's breakfast was a one-off, we were secondly surprised the next day. We could order what we wanted and it was served to us by the lovely lively nuns. And every day at 1200 hours, after morning lessons, we were served with dinners of steak and lamb and pork and gammon and potatoes and vegetables, along with Black Forest gateau that was so rich it made me sick because I'd never tasted it before and made a first-time pot-bellied pig of myself. It was like a holiday camp and I could happily have served out the rest of my two years there. In fact, I would've been willing to join the order if they'd asked me to and become a *hochwürden*.

Our spare time was spent exploring the dense forest around the retreat and it was breathtaking to a country boy like me. I'd never seen nothing like it in all my hill-trekking, absconding-over-the-wall days. I explored the trails and the tracks and got lost in the folklore of it. I saw Hansel and Gretel skipping secretly with their basket of breadcrumbs and Rapunzel's long hair tumbling down from the tree-tops and a snow-white girl biting into a blood-red apple and Rumpelstiltskin spinning in the gold evenings and all kinds of elves and gnomes and trolls and things

and they had to come and find me when it was time to go in. I
never saw any other local people out there in the folk-forest, only
the nuns. There was nobody else around and it seemed we were
no longer part of the real world and lived for a while inside the
imagination of some storyteller. There was no formality in the
medieval castle, we wore whatever we wanted to wear – even
though we only had our army uniforms. But we could walk in
shirt sleeves and bare feet and the nuns didn't mind and did all our
washing and food-and-watering for us and we did nothing at all.

Except dream.

Some of the bad lads teased the nuns when they came to wake
us in the mornings – especially the younger ones like me.

'Can you help me up please, sister?'

'Don't you want nun?'

Coarse and casual stuff like that. But it didn't bother them and
I'm sure they'd heard it all before from other silly soldiers. They
were good sports and took it all in their stride – either that or they
didn't understand the English innuendo and double entendre.
The last day was spent filling in our exam papers and, like I said,
the others all passed with cheating colours from copying me and,
in so doing, we earned ourselves an extra half-knicker a week.
And like an orb appearing in the forest for a brief flash, the ten
days were over and it was time to go. We said our goodbyes and
thank-yous to the nuns and I could have cried. I could have hung
on to the gates and had to have my fingers broken to make them
let go. I could have kicked and screamed and lay on the floor and
had to be dragged to the waiting lorry. I could have run off into
the woods and waited for the world to go away again. But I

didn't. And I left like the brave soldier I was – and tried not to look back.

It was hard to readapt to all the army bullshit and bluster after the retreat. But the football season soon started and the boxing and cross-country running, and my short span of attention was distracted away from the wonderment of the woods. I was good at all these sports and was picked to represent the Steelbacks in many tournaments, and that was another thing I had to thank my younger days in the reform schools for. But the mind-numbing army routines still had to be performed day in and day out and, although the sports provided some relief from the boredom, it still got into my bones. I think it was because I was never really cut out for army life and was only here because I had to be. I was always a bit of a maverick, bucking the system and running away and ending up on jankers or in the guardhouse. I wasn't one for the discipline or for the glad fool-suffering and I suppose I was a bit like my father in the latter respect. So I wasn't worried when my name was selected as a compulsory volunteer to go on Berlin Guard duty.

There was no Berlin Wall in 1952 – it wasn't constructed until 1961 – but after World War Two there was what was called the Inner German Border, which was the frontier between East and West Germany. It was heavily fortified on the Eastern or Soviet side, especially in the city of Berlin and, in 1952, the Soviets began erecting high metal fences with barbed wire and watch-towers and minefields and anti-vehicle ditches. There was one place in Berlin where the trains crossed over from west to east and back again and that was at Checkpoint Charlie. It was a tense place, with 50,000 Soviets and East Germans on one side and thousands of British, American and West German guards and soldiers on the other. All trigger-happily facing off and expecting war to break back out at any minute. Behind the front-line border, more than a million NATO and Warsaw Pact troops stood staunchly ready for any mad outbreak of hostilities. Although no one wanted another war, apart from the bomb-and-bullet makers, everyone was jumpy and jangly and jittery. And to make things even more manic, there were different zones on our side – like the British Zone and the US Zone and the French Zone – and they all converged on Checkpoint Charlie like it was a surgical strike target, with the GDR, or German Democratic Republic, on the other side, controlled by the Soviet Union strong-arms.

When trains came through the British Zone, going to the GDR, British soldiers were assigned as guards until the trains came to the border at Checkpoint Charlie Then we handed over responsibility to the Soviet guards, who took the train on into the GDR. The trains were passenger trains and we had to go through the carriages and check IDs for any kind of tinker, tailor, soldier or sailor who might be a spy. We didn't have a clue what we were looking for and if the picture on the ID looked like the person who was holding it, then it was alright – it could have been George Smiley or one of his moles for all we knew and we just wanted to get through our stag without causing an international incident that might result in the whole bloomin' world being blown apart. I was selected for a seven-day stint of duty on these trains and was sent over to Berlin from Wuppertal. I thought it would be a bit of an adventure and would break the monotony of barracks life. It was a long way to go and I had to pass through East Germany to get there. That was the strange thing about Berlin. It was right in the heart of East Germany, yet the western side of the city was controlled by the British and American and French military. Anything to make life leary, eh?

Up until 1952 we could still cross East Germany by train to get to West Berlin, but the Soviets started to tighten things up because they were losing too many citizens escaping to the wicked West, so flying in by plane soon became the only way into West Berlin. But for now, the trains were still running through the city from West to East and back again. There was a constant flow of *züges* and I'd get guard-dutied off one going into the Eastern sector only to be immediately boarded back on another going in the opposite direction. Back and forth, back and forth, through the British sector. Off one and on to another – on and off, on and off, for the whole time I was on that stag.

When I first arrived, I reported to the Berlin Guard barracks and was put on 24-hour guard duty for seven days – doing two hours on and two hours off. The problem was, us poor squaddies had only our old Lee-Enfield 303 rifles and we weren't allowed to have a round up the spout – in case, of course, it went off by accident and started World War Three. Whereas the Russians had AK-47s that were fully loaded and primed and ready for action at a second's notice. We were supposed to ask the officer in charge if we could load up in case of trouble and the answer was always, 'No!' Once we got to Checkpoint Charlie, we got off the train and the Russians got on. We said nothing nor did we make eye contact with them, because they looked a lot fiercer than us and we knew if anything went wrong, we'd be brown bread for sure. I reckon they knew full well we had no bullet up the spout and they had nothing to worry about and that made them strutting and arrogant and sneering at us. I wasn't normally nervous of much back then, but that situation scared some of the sauce out of me and I'm glad to say I was only selected for the Berlin Guard once and I never complained about being bored back in the barracks at Wuppertal again.

This close encounter with the Kalashnikovs encouraged me to try to lose my virginity once again. I didn't want to die without knowing what it was all about and I decided not to waste any more time, but to just get on with it. I went to the medic and asked for five French letters.

'How many you going to use?'

'All of them, I hope!'

So on the Saturday morning, after the usual parade, I went into Wuppertal with the sole intention of finding a prostitute and saying goodbye, once and for all, to my green-dick. I hoped I'd be able to go through with it, because it was starting to get my goat. I went into the first drinking bar I came to and looked around. It was full of soldiers, but no prostitutes. The only woman was the girl behind the bar, serving beer. I didn't want the squaddies to know what I was up to, because I'd have got some stick and it would've embarrassed me and I'd either have belted one of them or just put it off again and stayed there and got drunk. So I approached the young Fraulein barperson and ordered a pint. I bided my time until she had a quiet moment.

'You speak English?'

'Yes.'

'I want ... er, a lady of the night.'

'You vant old lady mit a kite?'

'No, no ...'

But she had to go back serving the soldiers and I had to wait for another quiet moment. That took some time and I was on my third pint before I got the opportunity again. Maybe she didn't understand me because I was whispering and she couldn't quite get my drift – or maybe she was just having a chuckle at my expense.

'I want someone to ... a prostitute?'

'You vant someone to press your suit?'

'For fuck's sake ...'

I held up one of the French letters and she smiled.

'Ah, you vant *eine Hure*!'

She said this out fairly loud and a lot of the lads looked round and I had to hide my face behind my hot hands. She told me to go out the door and turn left – down the street to the second house I came to and knock and say Ingrid sent me. I did the snake-shuffle out of the bar, trying not to look like I was in a big hurry, with all the sniggering eyes following me and pointing with laughing fingers. There were a lot of people in the street and they all seemed to be watching me. So I started whistling and went on down past the second door. Then I pretended I'd forgot something and came sauntering back – but kept on walking again. Then I turned round and passed it again and was starting to look like a simpleton and, if people weren't really watching me before, they were now! Every time I went to knock, it seemed like some bugger was on my shoulder, so I kept going. This went on for nearly half an hour and I finally told myself I had to either perform or get off the pot. So I went straight up to the door and banged on it, with my heart beating like a bongo drum and my legs ready to run. A woman of about thirty opened the door. She was sexy and shimmying and had a head of dark hair. But she wasn't smiling.

'Ingrid sent me.'

'Come in.'

She led me along a hallway and into a large room with a queue of randy blokes waiting with their tongues protruding and dripping cigarette-stained saliva on the linoleum.

'I saw you goink up und down. You should haf saved that fur the bed.'

Cheeky.

'How much will you charge me?'

'Five marks fur thirty minutes.'

Five marks was about 7s/6d, which was a lot out of my pound-a-week wages, and if I hadn't been getting the extra ten bob for being a good Catholic I might have paused at the price – but it was now or never. I nodded my head.

She told me to wait and she'd bring over the girls when they were ready and I could choose which one I wanted. But I didn't fancy doing it with someone who'd been shagged four or five times in the last hour by some big-knobbed BFGs.[12]

12 British Forces Germany.

'What about you? Do you do it?'

'*Ja*, but I thought you vant a young girl?'

'No, you'll do.'

She took me to a room and stripped off all her clothes and lay on the bed with her legs akimbo. I just stared at her out through my open mouth because I'd never seen a naked woman in that position before – except maybe in magazines. I was just about to drag my strides off when she raised her head.

'Money first.'

I remembered the last time I paid money up front to *Die Dirne* and came away with bugger all, so I wanted to be in position before I parted with the cash.

'I'll put the money on the table when I get my trousers off.'

Which took me a while, because I had the hunchback of all hard-ons and then I had to fit the Frenchie, which I had very limited practice in doing, and I could see she was getting a little impatient, which flustered me all the more.

But I finally managed it and stood there with the old chap safely encased in the French letter and shoved the five marks onto the little table. Then I lay on top of her, but nothing much happened.

'What do I do now?'

'Your first time?'

'Yes.'

'Hah. I vill show you.'

So she guided me in and after two pushes, that was it and I tried to pretend I hadn't come my coco so soon, but she knew.

'That is it, Tommy. Next time you vill know a bit more.'

I got off her and got the Frenchie off me and slipped back into my strides and left. It was a cold experience, not at all what I expected. Then I thought she might be a woman who had been raped at the end of the war like a lot of them were in Germany and she didn't really care for soldiers all that much, despite her profession. When I got back to camp I said to myself, 'What a waste of five marks that was.'

I never tried it again while I was in Germany.

9

Walking the Winklestrasse

The British Army of the Rhine (BAOR) had a boxing competition and all the battalions entered for it. It was a knockout event, though not necessarily literally, and I was picked to represent the Northamptonshires in the light-welterweight division. Our coach was Regimental Sergeant Major Smart, whose wife, if you remember, got me put on a fizzer for having potato knees when I was in Trieste. Smart never mentioned his missus to me after that incident and I steered clear of her and Mrs Whelan from then on. I was thinking the RSM probably knew his old lady was screwing a lot of squaddies, but he never let it interfere with his ring coaching – a true slug-trainer.

The Cooper twins, Henry and George, were in the same competition, fighting for the Royal Army Ordnance Corps, and everyone was hoping they wouldn't come up against the super-Coopers – as you know, Henry went on to become British, European and Commonwealth heavyweight champion and

George was just as good a boxer in his own right, though not as well known. The Steelbacks did very well in winning the first four rounds and getting to the quarter-finals – but then we came up against the Cameron Highlanders. I was doing good in my fight until the third round, when I walked into a jackhammer right to the jawbone. I was dizzy, but didn't go down, and it was adjudged I lost the fight on points.

I went straight to my bunk when I got back to barracks and the next thing I remembered was coming to in the military hospital. Apparently, they couldn't wake me at reveille and they put me on a charge for not getting out of the unconscious bed. When they realised something was wrong and I was either knocked out or suffering from narcolepsy, they took me to the hospital to find out which. I was concussed cold for forty-eight hours, and as soon as I woke up they declared me fit as a fighting cock and threw me out – no light duties or nothing. To add insult to injury, we lost the contest 8–9 and, as I was the only one beaten, it was all my fault. I felt gutted as a goose on Christmas Eve. But RSM Smart was more forgiving. He promised he'd take us on a weekend to Hamburg if we won the BAOR title and, fair play to him, he did just that – even though I'd let the side down by sleepwalking into the big right-hander.

By the way, the Cooper twins won the light-heavyweight and heavyweight titles for the Sugar Sticks in the tournament on that particular occasion.

The weekend in Hamburg was a right royal hootenanny of a holiday. We had this geezer with us called Sergeant Harry Oliver, who couldn't read English, never mind German, and we played all sorts of pranks on him. But you had to be careful with Harry and not push him too far, because he killed a man in a street fight in England and couldn't go back there or he'd end up in prison for manslaughter. So he stayed in the army, changing regiments every time his mob was due to go back home, always joining outfits that were stationed abroad – it didn't matter where to happy-fists Harry, as long as he could stay out of England.

Anyway, the whole weekend was paid for by boxing-club funds and was spent boozing and walking up and down the Winklestrasse, which is what we called the Reeperbahn, and looking at all the half-naked girls in the red-light windows and getting into punch-ups with the Cameron Highlanders. There was a permanent feud between the Steelbacks and the Camerons because of something that happened during the war and I never found out exactly what it was. I just knew that, whenever we met up anywhere, skin and hair would be flying. Some of the regulars and older guys went with the prozzies, but I steered clear. They were all telling stories after and I told my lies too, otherwise I'd get the mickey taken. But it was just a big bluff. And, anyway, I never fancied batting on a sticky wicket – apart from that one time in Wuppertal, when I chose the hen rather than one of the clucking chicks.

The regiment also entered the BAOR football tournament and, again, we made it into the quarter-finals – only to find we'd drawn another Scottish regiment, the Royal Scots. We kicked off the quarter-final at 1400 hours on a Saturday afternoon and at half-time we were 1–0 up and I'd scored the goal. I was a-cocking and a-crowing all over the pitch and I thought this would make up for being beaten in the boxing. The RSM gave us a half-time pep talk and told us to go out and score another quick goal in the second half and then just shut up the goal.

You're a brickie's apprentice, Sears . . . build a wall in front of it!'

That was the strategy then to win – except it didn't work out that way. The Scots brought on Jock Brown after the interval and this bastirt played part-time for Glasgow Rangers. They put him in at centre-forward and he scored two goals in as many minutes and four more over the rest of the half. From being 1–0 up at half-time, we lost 6–1 by the final whistle and the wall of wingers and strikers and sweepers in front of the goal made no difference to Jock – who went on to play full-time for Rangers and got capped for Scotland after being demobbed.

The Royal Scots went on to win the competition.

It was coming up to Christmas 1952, and about 300 of us from the Northamptonshires were told we were to be transferred to the Essex Regiment in the New Year. This was to make the Essex up to full battalion strength in preparation for being sent to Korea. We were transferred for more intensive training to Lunenburg Heath in Saxony, north Germany. It was a large area of heath and geest and woodland in the northeastern part of the state, close to Hamburg and Bremen, and we were back under canvas again, just like when we were up in the Alps at Klagenfurt. Some areas were so densely forested that very little light got through the trees and none at all after dark. As it was Christmas time, three of us booked out and hiked through the forest to a local *bierhaus* and got Brahms-and-Liszt. We lost our bearings on the way back and couldn't see a thing in the dark *bewalden*-black. We were stumbling around all over the place when we came across a small hand-built forester's hut. The forester was a former foot-soldier in the Wehrmacht and he only had one leg, but he put us up for the night on the floor of his hovel and when we woke late in the morning, we could see that our camp was only a hundred yards away and the bugger never told us. I got done for not booking back in on time and had to paint the grass purple. I could hear that forester laughing through his wooden leg.

Most of the time at Lunenburg was spent acclimatising ourselves with the weapons of war – like the anti-tank grenades we fired off the ends of our rifles. The recoil from these could break your shoulder, so we used to fire 'em swinging from a lanyard, which was very dangerous and if it swung or swong the wrong way you could end up looking for a job as a eunuch in a harem. We spent a month or so out on the wild German heath and that took me into 1953 and the last of my teenage years – not that there was any such thing as a teenager in those days. You went from being a boy to a man and I became a man the day I went to work for my father, after finally getting out of the reform schools.

After Lunenburg, I was given twenty-eight days' leave to go and see all the family back in Treacle Bumstead. I went with John Wells from Ebberns Road in Hemel Hempstead, and as soon as I got home my dear old dad asked if myself and John would like to work our four weeks' leave with him, instead of loppeting on the larch.

'When d'you want us to start?'

'Tomorrow.'

Next day, my father took us down to Lawn Lane in old Treacle Bumstead, where he was building a big garage. There was a beauteous big ash tree in the way, maybe forty foot high with a three-foot-thick trunk, and we were to cut it timber-falling down and then dig and concrete the footings and do the brickwork up to dampcourse level. FW was paying us a fiver a week and that was the best money the old skinflint had ever offered me. I could barely believe it. But he knew what he was doing, my dad. The work was hard and we only had three weeks to do it all in – that meant he'd get his garage built for thirty quid from rooftop to floor-bottom – a lot cheaper than if he got an outside crew in. And he knew it.

Trouble was, he only left us an old cross-cut saw that was used by Noah in the building of the Ark and an axe that was as blunt as a bag of wet mice, along with two shitty old shovels with broken handgrips and a couple of forks with prong-points missing. And I wished, right then, that we had the old Browning water-cooled heavy-machine-gun we buried back on the slopes of Schmeltz.

'What about a ladder?'

'There's one in the shed. I'll be back at six o'clock.'

The ladder was as rickety as a recycled bicycle, but we put it up against the tree and started to cut some of the branches off. It was a joke that had lost its punchline; the saw wouldn't cut through melted cheese and I had to traipse off to the local ironmongers to buy a new blade. While I was gone, I told John to go round to Dick Hemmings the blacksmith and get the axe sharpened. The new sawblade cost me 7s/6d and the axe sharpening cost 3s/6d – a total of eleven scarce shillings. I was now out of pocket, before we even started – and that was going to take a bite out of my first week's fiver.

My father came back at six o'clock and he wasn't happy. We'd only managed to cut about three or four branches down.

'I expected that tree to be long felled by now!'

'I had to buy a new sawblade, Dad ... and pay Dick to sharpen the axe.'

'Oh, alright ... but have it down by dinner-time tomorrow!'

Next morning, me and John decided to leave the rest of the branches where they were and just cut the toothy-leafed tree down in one go, from the base. The first thing was, don't forget, we were without any safety gear or gauge-proof glasses or harnesses or hard hats – nothing like that back in them old bullocking days. And the second thing was we weren't sure which way to fell the tree. If we felled it to the front, it would land across the road. If we felled it to the back, it would bring a building down. To the right was a wall and to the left was a penfold fence. We decided to fell it towards the fence, which we'd have to take down first, so's not to damage it. Once the fence was down, we started chopping a V-shaped wedge in the base of the trunk, about halfway through. Then we started sawing from the other side. At ten o'clock she was ready to topple and we shouted, 'Timber!' But the tree didn't fall – worse than that, it started listing towards the road. We ran round and propped the ladder up against it to stop it falling out onto the street, then it started listing back towards the building behind us. We ran round with the ladder and propped it again, then it listed forward again. We ran round with the ladder and propped it again. We looked like a couple of the Keystone Kops, moving in fast-motion and trying to topple the bloody tree towards the taken-down fence.

Just then, my father pulled up in his pickup and the tree started listing towards the lorry. He nearly had nine nervous breakdowns.

'Jesus Christ, Ken, what are you doing?'

'It won't fall where we want it to, Dad.'

While John Wells and I tussled with the tree, pushing it this way and that and back and forth and sideways, my father got a rope from the truck and lassoed one of the branches. Then the three of us began to pull the stubborn old ash in the direction we wanted it to fall. It finally belly-flopped in a shemozzle of splinters and flying leaves and caused no damage. My father wasn't happy, but he was glad I at least had the sense to take the fence down first. He threw his rope back into the truck.

'Get it all cleaned up by six. I'll be back then.'

'We'll burn it, Dad.'

'You will not! Just saw it all up and we'll take the timber up to Sunnyside and use it for winter fuel.'

Waste not, want not, eh – as long as someone else is doing the sawing! I told you he was a tight old taskmaster, my father. I got the eleven shillings back from him, but only after a lot of whinge-ing and whining and wrist-twisting.

Next day, me and John turned up to start the real work – we were to dig out the footings after my older brother Bill set the site out for us. We waited till 10:30 a.m., but no sign of Bill. I knew my father would go garretty if he came round and there was no work done, especially after the traumatic fiasco with the tree, so I decided to do it myself. I set out, using a makeshift square I made up from bits of wood, and ran the lines off from the main house and measured up the corners and drains and levels and falls. Then we dug the footing out and started knocking up the concrete by hand. I decided if we knocked it up dry and then added the water on top, it would take less time. I put up the first corner and traced the bond out to the farthest one, the same on the next one and then back to the first. We then built all four corners up to dampcourse level and that's how me and John got on with it without the help of horse nor hand.

We finished this work at 4:00 p.m. and, right on cue, brother Bill turned up. He wasn't happy that I'd done his job without waiting for him.

'You can't set out, Ken!'

'Check it if you want.'

'I will.'

'If it's wrong, I'll jack, and Dad don't have to pay me nor John.'

That's how confident I was. Bill thought he was the terrier's testicles because he was FW's favourite white-haired boy and could do no wrong – whereas I was the wilful one and always running before I could crawl. He checked the work and found I was spot-on the hand-spit but, needless to say, he never gave me no credit for it and probably told Dad he'd sorted it all out himself. Anyway, me and John just got on with it and built this garage up from dampcourse to plate level and then put the ceiling joists on. My other brother Dave and a fella called Bernard Gillespie pitched the roof and, by the time it was all done, me and John only had 96 hours left of our 28-day leave.

My father shook his head when I said that's all the work we were doing for him, because we wanted a few days dangling before going back to barracks. We earned fifteen quid apiece on that job, which was a lot more than our army pay, even including food vouchers. So we felt like a couple of blue-arsed millionaires and we bimbled around sightseeing on my motorbike – all the local places and as far away even as Windsor. Sometimes I'd drive and sometimes John would – especially if I'd had a few pints in the local pubs. But all too soon it was time to poodle on back to pongoland.

Me and John Wells on leave in 1952 around
the time of the tree incident.

When our leave was over, me and John were sent as part of an advance party to prepare our new barracks at Warley, Brentwood, ahead of the main regiment returning from Germany. It was mainly maintenance work, making sure the barracks was up to scratch as it hadn't been in use for a longish while. There was twenty-eight of us whose names came up for this detail and the rest of the regiment stayed in Lunenburg. John was made up to sergeant and I was his second-in-command, unofficially of course, and we gave ourselves 48-hour passes every weekend and skived off to Southend-on-Sea on the motorbike. If any of the others wanted passes, they had to pay us for them. It was a licence to print pound notes and we took full advantage.

Plenty of money meant plenty of boozing, mostly round the pubs in Southend, which was the closest toffee-apple town to Treacle Bumstead. We'd drive down on the motorbike and stay for the whole weekend. There was this piano bar called the Hole in the Wall and I used to sing songs on the microphone with the ivory-tickler. She was a woman in her fifties that some would have said was a bit mutton-in-moiré, but she played with a nice figure and her name was Ronnie, which was short for Veronica, and she asked me if I wanted to stay over at her place. So John went back to camp on the bus and I stayed. This became a regular routine every weekend and sometimes during the week as well. She was an oldish girl in the eyes of the nineteen-year-old I was then — but she played like a bloody fine fiddle and, by the time it was all over, I was no longer a two-pump chump.

When the rest of the regiment came back off leave, we were all sent on a fortnight's weapons training to Fingringhoe (known to us, of course, as Fingering Hoe) rifle and firing range. The Ruperts reckoned we needed practise using two-inch mortars and the new 3½lb grenade-firing anti-tank weapons that the Yanks called bazookas. They also taught us to use .45- and .38-calibre pistols for close-range hand-to-hand, and this was something I just couldn't get the hang of. I was useless with the pistols, not like the crack shot I was with the rifle. It was something to do with the recoil – I couldn't hit a cow in a cornfield from twenty paces and was a definite danger to myself and others. It was all out in the countryside with nothing for miles and miles, no pubs nor shops nor sheep-farms nor milkmaids nor anything else that would interest a herd of hot-blooded hooligans. Totally dire and desolate, and we were back under canvas as well – always under bloody canvas on manoeuvres. And the end of March in 1953 was cold as a penguin's pubes in the eight-man bell tents, full of snoring and farting and pissing about and enough fag smoke to clog up a coke-chimney.

After this little stint, we were sent to Stanford Battle Area – known as STANTA, for Stanford Training Area – in Norfolk, for another fortnight. This was to give us even more intensive training under war conditions and knock the flies and freckles off us. The area was a 30,000-acre wasteland of gorse-covered sandy heath and was run by the Operational Training and Advisory Group, OPTAG. The spiel said, 'This in-theatre training is designed for pre-deployment in a war zone,' and we already knew we were going to Korea with the Essex Regiment.

Needless to say, we were back under bloody canvas again and a good part of the training revolved round taking part in mock warfare with other regiments. We also had to traipse through mock minefields and evacuate the casualties who had their mock legs blown off. It was like an episode of the American TV series *M*A*S*H*, with helicopter drills and defensive shoots and patrolling perimeters and the reading of the rules of engagement for opening fire. We were also taught some stuff about the culture of the Far Eastern country we were going to and about environmental health and how not to get the clap – which we already knew about.

I soon got a bit pissed off with all this training, as most of it

The Steelbacks, 1953. I'm fifth from left.

was the same old thing over and over again. It was the end of April and about a fortnight before I was due to go to Korea and I knew I might get killed out there and I wanted to enjoy what little time I might have left. So myself and three mates decided to go on the trot for a few days. We knew we'd be put on a charge for being AWOL when they got hold of us, but what could they do – shoot us? We snuck out of the Stanford Battle Area when no one was looking and made our way back down to Brentwood Barracks. There wasn't much security in those days because there wasn't any terrorist threats from the IRA or Islamists or anything like that, and all you had to do was avoid the redcaps. It was as simple as strolling out the gate and getting on a bus and hopping on down the sixty miles or so to Essex.

When we got there that night, we broke into the NAAFI by means of me climbing up onto the roof and, being a builder, knowing how to remove a few tiles and break a few batons and swing down inside. But I accidentally banged my balls against the cash register as I dropped down, and rolled about the floor in pain, trying to hold the howls in, before I could get up and open the door for the others. Nobody noticed because the perimeter guards were probably asleep and, if they weren't, they were looking for people getting out over the fences and not too bothered about what was going on inside. We stole as many cigarettes and cigars and boxes of chocolates as we could fit into our kitbags – 10,000 fags, 500 cigars and 20 boxes of chocs. I let the others out the door and locked it from the inside. Then I climbed back on the roof without denting my goolies again, straightened out the batons as best I could and replaced the tiles. The NAAFI wallahs would never know they'd been broken into, because they were all on the fiddle and, if some merchandise was missing, they'd just assume one of them took it and it wouldn't get reported.

We decided to take this gear to the East End of London and flog it. So we hopped on a train from Brentwood into Leyton and shuffled into the first big pub we came to and had a whisper into the landlord's lughole. He took me quietly into his office, while the others stayed outside in the bar. Then he had a look at the bag of swag.

'I'll give you a shilling a packet for the fags.'

'Alright.'

'The same for each cigar.'

That would come to fifty quid and I was very well pleased.

'I don't really want the chocs, but I'll give you a fiver for the lot.'

I took his offer without even a haggle or a handshake, on condition he gave us four free pints of his best beer, which he did. We drank the bitter and left and I've never seen him or his pub from that day to this.

We split the money four ways and headed off to the pleasure palaces of the East End of London to have a good time. Having a 'good time' mostly meant getting pissed and staying pissed until the money ran out. We moved around the area, from Stratford to Bow to Stepney, and we slept in churchyards like I used to do back in the old days with Lillywhite. Spending that much money took a lot of drinking and we bought booze for everybody we came across and were very popular percy-pongos. There was no fighting or skin-flaying and we stayed out of trouble because we knew the Old Bill would just hand us straight over to the redcaps if they were called. The spree lasted three days, before we were all broke, so we made our way back to Brentwood Barracks and gave ourselves up, and my hungover head was waiting for the six-of-the-best and the loss of privileges for forty days. It was Monday morning and we were thrown into the cells and charged with being AWOL and were to be brought before the Battalion Commanding Officer on the Thursday. But, as we were due to sail for Korea in seven days, I reckoned there wasn't all that much he could do to us.

Even though we were in different cells, we were allowed to eat together and the others were worrying like women about what was going to happen to 'em.

'What's gonna happen on Thursday?'

'Don't worry about it.'

'Why not, Ken?'

'Because we won't be here.'

They looked at me like a parliament of owls that had landed on a live electric cable, and I said, 'I'm having another fling before they send me sailing to Korea.'

'But, we're in the guardhouse.'

'We can easy get out of here.'

They looked at each other for a minute or two and I waited while their heads spun round full circle and they found their lost voices.

'Can we, Ken?'

'This is what we'll do . . .'

Early on the Thursday morning, I called one of the guards to

let me out to the toilet. When he unlocked the cell door, I grabbed
hold of him and knocked him clean out with a hard right-cross
to the head. I took his cap and belt and tunic, then I got the keys
and let the other lot out of their cells. We snuck into the guardroom and overpowered the other two key-keepers and took their
caps and belts and tunics as well – because *they* took *our* belts and
caps and tunics when we were banged up, and if we were seen
walking around improperly dressed, we'd be arrested again and
hit with several flying books. We took the guards' money and
paybooks for the ID we'd need in case we got stopped. Then we
locked all three of them in my cell. Now we had three belts and
three caps and three tunics and three paybooks – between four of
us.

Just then, a sergeant came strutting in.

'What's going on 'ere?'

So we jumped him and took his tunic as well as his belt and
cap and money and paybook and locked him in a separate cell.
We knew we had about an hour to get clear of the camp before
the other guards out on patrol came back and freed the four sur-
rogate prisoners, so we shifted ourselves. Between them, the three
guards and the sergeant had £18/10s on them and we made our
way to the Southend-on-Sea arterial road and began thumbing a
lift. After about five minutes, a Sunbeam-Talbot 90 Mark II sports
car stopped. We ran up to it and saw it was being driven by a lieutenant in our own regiment.

'Where you going, sergeant?'

I didn't know who he was talking to for a few seconds, then
I realised I was wearing the guard sergeant's tunic. I didn't want

to say we were heading for Southend, because that would have sounded suspicious. We were a long way from there and it was a seaside resort and the first thing that would come into the Lewy's head was that we were going AWOL and wouldn't be back. Better to say we were visiting families.

'Hemel Hempstead, sir.'

'I'm going to Luton. I can drop you at St Albans.'

'That'll do us.'

So we all hopped into the sports car and took off like Stirling Moss at the Monte Carlo Rally.

'You boys have left it a bit late to be going home?'

'We've been on duty, sir. This is our last chance to visit our families before Korea.'

'Good lads. Same here.'

He was a pleasant enough chap, the Lewy. Little did he know that he was aiding the escape of four fugitives from the cells who'd just assaulted a sergeant and three guards. I wonder if he ever found out? When we got to St Albans, he wished us well and drove off towards Luton. We headed for the nearest café and, after a full-on feed, we double-timed it into a pub called the Fighting Cocks and had a few pints in there first. Then on to the Farriers and a few more. We hit as many pubs as we could before chucking-out time, then bought fish'n'chips before bedding down for the night.

'Where we gonna sleep, Ken?'

'Graveyard.'

I got the electrocuted owl look from them again and I had a job convincing them that it was the safest place to be when you're on the run. So we headed for the churchyard at St Albans Cathedral and finished our fish'n'chips and said our prayers before cuddling up to the crypts and sleeping the sleep of the dead – that only comes to men who are full to the gills of beer and greasy grub.

After a few days on the run and sleeping rough, we woke to the Sunday-morning clanging of bells in our banging heads and traipsed to the local public toilets to have a wash and brush-up. We wandered about until a café opened and stayed there drinking cups of tea until the pubs pulled the towels off the pumps and we could go back into the Fighting Cocks again. This time the landlord gave us a sideways look and asked us if we were the four soldiers who broke out of the army nick. We laughed nervously – 'Of course not!' – as he threw a newspaper at us. It was only the *News of the World* and the story was all over the front page – luckily without any pictures. It was in all the other national newspapers too and the landlord leaned menacingly over our table.

'Is it you lot?'

'I told you it ain't!'

I looked back at him even more menacingly and he stood off us.

'I didn't think so . . .'

'We're on weekend leave before going to Korea to fight against communism, mate.'

'In that case, have a drink on the house.'

We had his free drink and then drifted on down to the Portland Arms and told the same story and had another free drink and a game of darts. And that's how the Sunday morning moved along until chucking-out time at 2:00 p.m. Then we went to a café and spent the last of the guards' money on another good feed. There was nowhere else to go, so we sauntered over to the police station and gave ourselves up. And I know you won't believe this but, as luck would have it, the first copper we came across was my Uncle Alec, who I told you used to drive King George about.

'What you doing here, Ken?'

'Giving myself up. We're the boys who broke out of the army nick in Brentwood.'

'I thought you might be involved, Ken. Why d'you keep doing things like this?'

I listened to his lecture about how I was letting my mother and father down, and my brothers and sisters and all the chuckens in Hertfordshire as well. Then he arrested us and said he'd make arrangements to get us back to barracks. I told him he'd better hurry, because we're sailing for Korea at midday on Monday.

Like I said before, Alec was alright – for a copper. As an ex-military man himself, he knew if he kept us in the cells overnight and we missed the troopship to Korea, we'd be charged with desertion instead of AWOL and it would go hard for us. A court-martial could mean at least two years in a tough-arsed glasshouse like Colchester or Aldershot and we'd still have to do the rest of our National Service when we got out. Even though it was Sunday afternoon, Uncle Alec organised for a police car to drive us back to Brentwood in the gathering gloaming.

'By the way, how long you been a sergeant, Ken?'

'Since yesterday.'

'One day they'll bang you up and throw away the key.'

But he made sure we had a meal before we got taken away by the cop-car and we arrived back in Brentwood barracks at 2100 hours that night. We were immediately thrown back into the cells and, as luck would have it, the guards weren't the same ones we belted – otherwise we'd have got a good going-over. They didn't have time to court-martial us and I knew from Alec that, once outside the three-mile coastal limit, a ship's captain can't court-martial an infantry soldier – all he can do is give you twenty-eight days in the brig.

The next day, we'd be on a ship heading for Korea and the captain's authority would overrule all the army officers'.

Left to right, Peter Coxhill, John Wells and me on leave
and having a laugh just before Korea.

Shirt Lifting and Belly Shifting

Mad Bill Kelly never made it back to Korea. When the time came to join the Essex Regiment and get ourselves out there, he was considered to be too old. I had a last night on the beer with him in Wuppertal and I never saw him again after that. Although I still think about him – even now. And I hope he's sat back fishing somewhere in the starry sky, with a carton of ciggies and a six-pack by his side.

Next morning the four of us prisoners were handcuffed and taken, under armed escort, down to Southampton in a truck. The guards had a bit of a laugh with us about what we did, because they weren't regimental police or redcaps, who had no sense of humour whatsoever. We were dumped down in the cells, which were situated at the lowest level in the bow of the troopship *Asturias* – an old bucket that was built in 1925 and had seen a lot of action in World War Two. But now it was repainted in troopship colours – all white, with a coloured rib band round the hull and a yellow funnel. You probably won't remember, but the same ship starred in the 1958 film *A Night to Remember*, about the *Titanic*. But that was no consolation to us prisoners stuck deep down in its stinking hull at that time – even if we'd known about it.

One thing I forgot to mention, back when I was in Lunenburg, for some unknown reason my name came up on Battalion Orders to be made into a lance corporal and then to a full corporal before I got out to Korea. A lot of NCOs were throwing in their tapes before going out there, because they didn't want to get the first bullet from the men they'd bullied for so long. Many of them probably did get shot for being the right scumbags they were – even without their stripes. I told them I didn't want the responsibility of a chevron, the ones who were taking the extra pay in peacetime should be made to do the job in wartime as well. But they said they were going to send me on an NCO course whether I wanted to go or not. I told the officer in charge that I'd deliberately fail every test they gave me and he said it didn't matter, they'd make me up to a corporal anyway. But I dug my heels in and it was a bit of a battle, but I point-blank refused to go on the course and, in the end, they gave up on me and sent some shoe-licker instead. But, I mean, why would they want to make a glasshouse good-for-nothing like me into a corporal? They must've been bloody desperate! Other than that, I didn't mind going to Korea, despite what had happened to Bill Kelly out there – but a lot of others did!

In May 1953 the Essex Regiment, with me down in the dungeon, embarked from Southampton on the troopship *Asturias*, en route to Korea, as part of a Commonwealth Army fighting with the US against Chinese and North Korean communist 'aggression'. We were well out to sea before they dragged us up into the air and we went before the Battalion Commander. The proceedings were presided over by the ship's captain and we were charged with breaking out of the guardroom – nothing else. We got given the regulation twenty-eight days in the hole, instead of a court-martial, and we let out a silent harmonious sigh. The Battalion Commander wasn't impressed, but there was nothing he could do.

Sears had struck lucky again!

Being down at the bottom of the ship, at the front end, was like riding a surfboard in a submarine. We could feel every wave as the bow cut through the water and we were battered about like cod in a chip shop. It took getting used to for the first day and a couple of the lads were as sick as drowning sea-dogs. We never had no light nor air and the grub they gave us smelled like that stuff they throw over the sides of shark-hunting chum-ships. But that was the easy bit. By the evening of the second day, we were well into the Bay of Biscay and the weather got really rough. We were thrown about like rag dolls at a bull terriers' tea-party and the cell walls were pebble-dashed with vomit. This went on till we reached Gibraltar and cruised through the Strait into the Mediterranean. Things settled down as we sailed along the coast of North Africa and we finally docked for the first time at Port Said. They let us out of the brig and up on deck and it was good to get some clean air into my lungs again. I thought they'd throw us back down in the hold for the rest of our twenty-eight days, but they didn't. We were still under open arrest and not allowed any shore leave and we were banged back up in the cells at 2100 hours every night till 0600 hours next morning. Other than that, we could get up on deck for the free air.

The *Asturias* was docked about half a mile out from the port and it wasn't long before the bumboats came paddling out, selling all kinds of stuff: fruit and watches and cheap jewellery and hats and young girls – and the sound of them shouting up at us was like a chorus of starlings back in England, when they migrate over from Europe to roost for the winter. We were glad to be out of the stink and vomit of the cells, watching it all. The soldiers and sailors would see what they wanted and the goods would come up in a basket on a rope and the money would go back down the same way to the bumboat. One bloke from the regiment was leaning out of a porthole and made the mistake of sending his cash down first, but the stuff he bought never came back up. He was screaming holy murder at the bumboy and the little joker threw a knife at him. It went straight through the porthole and parted his hair. So the squaddie ran up on deck and got hold of the nearest ship's bowser and aimed it into the small skiff. He turned it on and the force of the water sank the boat. The NCOs grabbed him and he was confined to his bunk until the ship sailed at midnight. But it was too late for the bumboy. He had to swim to his nearest neighbour to get back to shore and I suppose he had to come out later and try to haul up his boat and merchandise.

Apparently, this was a common occurrence at Port Said.

The *Asturias* sailed into the Suez Canal at midnight and next morning, after breakfast, we went back on deck to see what

Egypt was like. I imagined a land full of sand and camel shit and flies and I wasn't far wrong. We had a lot of servicewomen and children on board, wives of men stationed abroad who were going to join their husbands in places like Singapore and Hong Kong and Aden. The local riff-raff gathered on the banks of the Red Sea and pulled up their long-shirts and showed everything they had, all a-swinging and a-dangling down. They shouted over to the women:

'Lookie, lookie, want a fuckie?'

'Lady want a fuckie?'

An officer called out, 'Put a few rounds over their heads.'

This had the desired effect and everything settled back down until the next lot started flashing further down.

After the canal, our next stop was Aden, in the Yemen, and we'd been at sea for about seven days. I wasn't allowed shore leave on account of being under ship's arrest, but I paid some bloke ten bob to get me a shore pass in his name, because I was sick of the sea swell and wanted to stand on solid ground for a short while. Now, I thought I'd seen everything, but I'd never seen a place like Aden before. The goat was the sacred animal of the area – I think it had something to do with its testicles, like one male goat being able to cover 150 females, and when the Romans controlled the place, they used to tear goats apart and eat them alive to give them the power of sexual perversion. Something like that – I never found out for sure. Anyway, Aden was alive with goats. The smelly tin-can-eaters were everywhere, allowed to go everywhere – into shops and cafés and houses – and the bloody goat shit was shin deep.

Anyway, I was walking along having a look at the place, when this Arab came up and spoke to me in a hoarse accent.

'Hey, Tommy, you want to see sexy show?'

He looked a bit fierce, like he had one of them curved knives tucked into his long-shirt and would slit my throat in a second if I said no.

'Er . . . alright.'

'Cost fifty riyal.'

'Er . . . alright.'

He took me to a nearby tent with about thirty other soldiers in there already, presumably after paying their fifty riyal too, which was about 2s/6d in real money. Then this Arab woman came in, and she was covered up with a long dress and a veil and we didn't know what to expect. But she dropped the dress and kept the veil and a huly-huly underskirt and started doing a belly dance and a-shaking her arse about all over the place. It was tame compared to what we'd seen in other places and the soldiers soon got a bit irate after parting with their fifty riyal. She was a big woman and could certainly shift herself and her belly, but we couldn't even see her face, never mind the interesting bits of her, and maybe it was sexy to the long-shirts but to the rest of us it was like watching your mother doing the rumba.

It didn't take long for things to take a turn for the worse – beer cans started flying first, then chairs and clumps of donkey shit. The long-shirts didn't like this infidelic intolerance and others came a-running into the tent and a full-scale riot soon broke out, with fists and boots and teeth a-flying and people being swung round by the tails of their shirts and others by their hair and some by their beards and, the worst of it all was, I wasn't even supposed to be ashore in the first place. I thought the best thing to do was duck down on all fours and ferret my way over the bodies and broken bones to the tent-flap, and then away from that place before the MPs got there to finish what the squaddies had started.

I was glad to get back on the boat.

Before we left Aden, we noticed a big black cloud coming towards the ship. Nobody knew what it was – but we soon found out. It was my first face-to-face with a swarm of locusts – millions of big ugly flying grasshoppers. Within seconds, everything was covered; they came sheeting out of the sky and grew on the bodies of the men who were up on deck watching the cloud coming with their ignorant open mouths. The ship wasn't made of steel any more, but green tissue and eyes and legs and antennae. The bloody things were three inches long and the noise of their wings was deafening – I never heard nothing like it before and I haven't since. The captain set sail straight away. He knew the insects would leave as soon as we started to move away from the land, where their food source was. I caught a big one and pulled its wings off and took it below to my bunk and tied a length of cotton round it like a dog lead. Back on deck, the rest of the locusts were gone, but a few of the other soldiers had the same idea as me and we were leading our locusts round like little pets. Then some bright spark suggested we should have an insect race over ten yards and a book was made with bets taken and a prize of five shillings for the winner. Now, my locust was bigger than the others and I was confident he'd win, so I put several shillings on it and so did a few others. But size isn't everything and the big bugger came last. One of the bad losers stamped a disgruntled foot on it and shouted, 'It won't lose again, Ken!'

I had to agree.

One of my mates from Treacle Bumstead who I joined up with was also on board the *Asturias*. His name was Dave Griffiths and he was a big strong boy who worked as a farm labourer back in Apsley End, so he was well used to being out in all weathers and his skin was as tough as horse-tack. Anyway, Dave fell asleep on deck and it was so hot that his back was burned red-raw when he woke up. It was one big blister, from his neck to the top of his tail bone. He knew if he went to sickbay he'd be put on a charge for self-inflicted wounding – like if you got drunk and couldn't make reveille, or got a dose of the pox. So he came to me and asked if I'd put some ointment on his back to ease the pain. Not knowing how bad the burn was, I agreed to do it and told him to get in the bunk and lie on his belly. Well, when I saw his back it made me feel sick. The blister completely covered it.

'You need to go to sickbay with this, mate!'

'No, Ken, they'll throw me in the brig.'

'Well, I'll have to pop it before I can put anything on it.'

'Just do it, Ken. I'm in agony.'

So I did. And about a pint-and-a-half of liquid flowed out and the smell of it nearly shrivelled my sinuses. Anyway, I covered his back with ointment and then cut one of my cotton vests up the sides to each armhole and covered the cream with it. I got some plasters out of my housewife and stuck the corners of the vest to Dave. Next morning, before breakfast, I checked to make sure it wasn't getting infected, then I dressed the burn again, same way as before. I knew Dave wouldn't be able to answer muster call, so I told him to stay in his bunk and I'd do it for him.

'Griffiths!'

'Yar.'

I did that for three days. And, because I was on ship's arrest, if I'd got caught, I'd probably have been keelhauled. On the second day, Dave's back began to scab up and go dry. I used more cream to soften it and scraped off the scabs where I could. On the third day, it started to get back to normal, although it was several different shades of strawberry. But at least he could make the muster.

We sailed out into the Arabian Sea and I saw the guards from Stanford who we'd duffed up. But they were alright about it though and didn't bear no grudges. The sergeant even came over and shook my hand and said I had guts and I'd make a good fighting soldier out in Korea. After ten days or so at sea, we sailed over the equator on our way south past the Maldives and the sailors did the crossing ceremony. They dressed up as King and Queen Neptune and they made a pool out of canvas, about twenty-five foot square and three foot deep. This was filled with seawater and all kinds of rotting food and rubbish and it smelled like a sea-dog's arse after seven days shore leave. We had to go through it head first, with our hands behind our backs, and then kiss Queen Neptune's fanny – which was a pot scourer stuffed down a back-to-front G-string on the ugliest sailor aboard ship. Once you were down there, your face got shoved into the scourer, which took the skin off your nose. The band played sea shanties all the time the ceremony was going on, which was most of the day, and we were given a single shot of rum from the NAAFI on-board canteen, which I traded for a bottle of beer. It was good fun, but I didn't want to repeat the experience and was glad it was night and I was safely thrown back in my cell when we crossed over again on our way to Colombo in what was then the island of Ceylon.

The heat was well over a hundred degrees in what shade we could find and you could fry albatross eggs on the deck. Yet it was better to be up there in what breeze there was, rather than down in the stifling and sweating below. This part of the trip was slow and boring because there was no land in sight for some time and the heat was exhausting without even doing anything at all. A few days out and we were told a show was going to be held on the stern of the ship that night. I decided to go and have a look, just to break the monotony. The crew were all merchant seamen and they had their own band and they were playing all the popular songs of the day – like 'I Believe' and 'How Much Is That Doggy in the Window?' and 'She Wears Red Feathers and a Huly-Huly Skirt' and all the other hit-paraders. They had three girls with them and you could have a dance for a shilling. One lad tried copping a handful while he was doing the quickstep and got a belt in the belly for his trouble. So a shilling was a bit steep if there was only a dance and nothing else coming with it – like a smooch or something to take back to the bunks with us. Apart from the navy rum, the booze on board was mostly Tiger beer, which was brewed in Malaysia and was as strong as rhinoceros urine. Other than that, if you wanted, it was Red Shield or White Shield, which were both just as strong as the Tiger, and the White Shield stayed fermenting in the bottle – so the longer it was left, the stronger it got. And you never drank the sediment, or you'd be pissing out your arse for a fortnight. But I had a good time and the show went on every other night while we were out there in the Indian Ocean.

During the day, we had target practice off the stern, firing our 303 Lee-Enfields at blown-up balloons. Being a crack shot with a rifle, I was one of the first to have a go. Nobody could hit a balloon because they were being blown about all over the place by the breeze and the swell from the ship. I fired off five rounds and only managed to hit one. But the sergeant said I'd done well, better than anyone else. I soon sussed out that the best way to hit the target was to wait till it rose to the top of a wave and was static for just a fraction of a second. Next time I had my turn, I shot three balloons – which was a record. We also had a sort of sports tournament, which was voluntary, and one of the events was deck-running. The races were anything from a hundred yards to a mile. I took part in the 800 and 1,500 metres, but never won any of them because it was too damn hot and I took my time jogging round. But it broke up the boredom of a long sea voyage with bugger-all to do except fry on the deck or dehydrate down below.

Now, Treacle Bumstead is an inland town and nowhere near the sea, so I was amazed at seeing flying fish for the first time, and porpoises jumping out of the water and eating them in full flight. Such sights made me wonder at the diversity in the world and appreciate that there was much more on this planet than most people ever get to see. I'd cursed the army for dragging me into it and interrupting my apprenticeship, but now I started to realise that I would never have seen some of the things I did if I hadn't been inconvenienced like that and I wouldn't appreciate life the way I do nor would I look at things from the perspective I do without that war in the far Far East. So there was something to be said for National Service, but not too much because I don't want you to think it should be brought back again or anything.

By now we'd come back up over the equator again and were getting close to the west coast of Indonesia. The *Asturias* was on a course to sail down the Strait of Malacca and dock at Singapore. That's when the placid waters of the Indian Ocean turned nasty and we bore the brunt of some very big seas and some wicked weather. I went from being able to sleep up on deck to being nearly washed off it by the huge waves that were breaking over the side of the ship. What they didn't tell us is that the Indian Ocean is the warmest ocean in the world and summer storms are severe, with the monsoon bringing strong southwesterly winds between May and October – so we sailed right into the start of it as we approached Indonesia. But, luckily for us jelly-legged land-lubbers, we were close to the strait and the coasts of Malaysia and Indonesia sheltered us on either side once we got in there.

Then, one morning, it was announced over the tannoy that the new Queen was about to be crowned and all ships of the British Navy should splice the mainbrace on 2 June to celebrate the occasion. Now, I didn't know what 'splice the mainbrace' meant and I thought there would be some kind of rope-tying ceremony or something, like when we crossed the equator. We were told to take our mugs up on deck and we were given a double ration of navy rum. Well, I'd never drunk real rum before and this stuff was thick and black and 140 per-cent proof and it smelled like something in between tar and treacle. Us soldiers had our mugs filled and we went back down below decks to drink it. But as soon as I took a taste, I spat it back out and was going to slop the 'orrible stuff down the sluice – and I wasn't the only one. Then I had an idea.

'Pour it in my water bottle and I'll see if I can sell it to the merchant seamen.'

A few of us filled up several water bottles and I started selling it at a shilling a gill to the sailors and to any soldier who had a taste for the thick black stinky-stuff. And some did, once they got in the swing of things at the parties on the back of the boat. I made a fair bit of money, which we planned to spend as soon as we got to Singapore. Only one problem, I was still on ship's arrest and wouldn't be given no shore leave. I thought about paying some bloke ten bob to get me a pass in his name, but everyone wanted to go and see Singapore and nobody wanted to stay on the ship.

Then Dave Griffiths came to me.

'I want to return the favour, Ken.'

'What favour, Dave?'

'For sorting my back out.'

So he got a shore-leave pass in his name and gave it to me.

'I'll do the same when we get to Hong Kong, Ken.'

Apart from helping me out, Dave had met and married his girlfriend on embarkation leave before we sailed for Singapore, so he was still in love and not all that interested in the wine and the women of shore leave. But I was. When we docked, me and the boys who'd contributed their ration of rum went ashore for the six hours allowed and I paid for everything – the wine and the women! It was one of the best times I ever had in my life. Only trouble was, because the shore leave was so short, we couldn't go nowhere but the harbour area, which was rough as a boatswain's beard and twice as tough – full of corporals and coolies and sailors and strumpets, and I had to be on my best behaviour and not get caught up in no rows or ructions or I'd be thrown in the brig for the rest of the trip.

Back on board, we set sail with hung-over heads up the South China Sea towards the island of Hong Kong. But that sin-city wasn't exactly where we were going – no, we were going to Kowloon Peninsula instead on the lower tip of mainland China. And China was a much different place back in them days than it is now. Dave got me another shore-leave pass and I went into the walled city with the rest of them. But the other soldiers were only interested in trying to get the ferry across to Hong Kong, where the real action was. I didn't want to do that because I only had six hours to see the sights and I was in enough trouble without getting back late to the ship. It would've put Dave on the spot as well and I didn't want that. So I stayed in Kowloon and got merry on Tiger beer and some of the spirits they called Scotch whisky, with the labels spelled wrong and that's how you knew it was their own brew and not the proper Highland stuff. I also bought two erotic books – one called *A Night in a Moorish Harem* and the other called *The Autobiography of a Flea*. Both were banned in England and I paid one Hong Kong dollar for the pair. After I read them, I could've put a pair of hinges on the bunk sheet, so

I decided to rent them out to other soldiers. I charged a shilling a time but, after doing the rounds, they got into the hands of sex-maniacs from some other regiment and that was the last I saw of them. I often wondered where they ended up. Still, I more than doubled the money I paid for them – and I learned a few things about fornication into the bargain.

The next stop was Pusan Harbour in South Korea.

11

Swimming on the Side of a Hill

We disembarked to the stars-and-stripes sound of an American army band, playing their jazzed-up interpretation of 'Scotland the Brave' or 'Men of Harlech' or something that only the Yanks would think was essentially English. And that's not knocking the Scots or the Welsh; it's just an example of the Yanks not knowing their arses from their euphoniums. I didn't have much time for them after seeing Dresden and after one of our lads getting hit on the head with a smoke bomb at Trieste. An officer was spouting out a load of bullshit in a blue-grass accent.

'Welcome to Korea, you brave British soldiers.'

And I said to myself, 'Yeah, we're the ones who've turned up late this time, like you buggers in the two world wars.'

Anyway, we all had to go to the transit camp and get signed in at a hatch called a keyhole. The one I went to was being run by one of the lads I signed up with, Bob Wellings from Berkhamsted.

Such a small world! I stopped to have a chat with Bob and the queue behind me came to a standstill. They all started shouting and throwing things and Bob told me I'd have to move on and he hoped to see me when we both got back home. I said I hoped so too.

But I never did.

Next morning, after breakfast, we boarded this train made up of cattle trucks that was to take us to the front line, over the 38th parallel, which was to be our final destination. Before we got properly under way, the train pulled forward out of the station and stopped again and I looked out the window onto a dirt road. A young, pregnant Korean woman was obviously in difficulty and then, just like that, she squatted down and had the babby, right in front of my eyes. Nobody helped her. Everyone walked past as if she wasn't there, as if this was an everyday occurrence and nothing was out of the ordinary. I thought my eyes were playing poker with me for a minute and I wondered to myself what I was doing in this country that was as alien to me as the moon. It was the first time I'd ever seen a brand-new babby being born – apart from when I first flew out into the world myself. Later in life I was to see my own daughter emerging from her mother in our front room and it was the most moving thing I ever experienced. And seeing my daughter Heather being born took my mind back to Korea and I wondered if that little roadside babby survived.

I hope it did.

The train journey to the front took two full days and nights, across a landscape that looked like a barren wilderness to me, except for the hills. Korea was full of hills – hill after hill after hill and no flat ground at all. A hundred thousand black-and-blue forgotten hills! Once we left the train station at Pusan Harbour, I don't remember seeing any towns or villages and very few people – just the odd old man with an oxcart moving along a dirt track and nothing else except a couple of isolated British aerodromes and bushes and sparse vegetation and nothing worth growing in the rotting paddy fields. The war had been going on for three years, back and forth across the country, and everything was blown to bits and buggered.

The train was only going about twenty miles an hour and kept stopping and starting and we weren't allowed off except to queue with our mess tins at the field cookhouse for canned sausages and tomatoes. Other than that brief break, we were crowded sixty men to a truck and sitting on slatted wooden benches with sore arses. And it was baking hot – over a hundred degrees inside the roasting rail-trucks. We disembarked from the train when we ran out of railway track and we were shunted into a fleet of three-ton trucks, which drove us up close to our lines on a big hill. The area was known as the Kansas Line, just ten miles above the 38th parallel. But maybe I'd better explain a bit about the Korean War here, so you'll know better what I'm talking about?

The 38th parallel is a circle of latitude in the northern hemisphere and it separates North Korea from South Korea. In 1950, five years after the end of World War Two, the North Korean People's Army crossed the 38th parallel and invaded South Korea. As America was clinically psychotic about the spread of communism – and the people who make the bullets and bombs needed another enemy after the Nazis were defeated – they got involved. US troops were already in Japan after the war, so it was a short step across the sea to South Korea. Then China heaved herself in to help the North Korean communists and things got hairy. Fighting was fierce in the first year of the war, with advances and retreats and back-and-forths and to-and-fros and a few major battles. But by the beginning of 1953, the fighting had lapsed into a kind of stalemate and most of what was going on was just patrolling the lines and local skirmishes and raids and small sorties for outposts in no-man's land. Sometimes things hotted up a bit, with artillery duels and ambushes and hill battles, and in June, just about the time I got there, the North Koreans and Chinese launched regimental attacks and tried to gain as much ground as they could before an impending armistice. On 27 July 1953, about six or seven weeks after my arrival, the armistice was signed and all the fighting stopped. Now, I'm not claiming credit for this, it was just a coincidence I got there when I did – or was it?

We were billeted in eighteen-man marquees and we made our own beds out of sandbags and angle iron and tying wires. We put brush from the surrounding area on the angle-iron frames then palliasses filled with straw on top of the brush and our sleeping bags on top of the straw mattresses. It might not sound like it, but it was quite a snug bug-infested arrangement. For the first few weeks after arriving in Korea, most of my time was spent toing and froing between what used to be the front line and the more cautious Kansas Line, moving unused equipment back in case the armistice talks failed and we had to fight again from the new positions – ammunition and heavy machinery and everything and anything. What we couldn't move, we destroyed so the enemy wouldn't get hold of it if things went tits up. The Kansas Line was made up of a mixture of minor lines like American and us British and Canadian and New Zealand and Australian and Turkish and United Nations. During the talks, it was agreed that each side would move their troops back two kilometres from the front line and create a buffer zone. The Kansas Line was where we moved back to and the North Koreans and Chinese moved back the same distance on the other side. It was the 'uneasy' period of the Korean War – nobody knew if there would be a permanent ceasefire or not. And, even when it came, things were still 'uneasy' – still are to this day because, even though the ceasefire was agreed, the final terms of the armistice never were.

Anyway, you have the gist of the situation and the general grounds for me being there in the godforsaken first place. The main front line was clear across the whole country and was covered in camouflage netting that was fifteen foot high. It was like being under a great green and brown umbrella and it was so hot we worked in just berets and shorts and boots and socks, with putties wrapped round from the top of the boot to the calf – to stop the snakes from slithering up our khakis. We had a company of South Korean soldiers attached to our regiment – KATCOMs, for Koreans Attached To Commonwealth Forces. A few of them spoke English with an Asian accent and I soon became good friends with them. I helped them with their English and they gave me the gen on how to get by in the field – and make a few bob on the side. Now, the South Koreans were only earning a shilling a

week and they wanted to boost their wages, so the market forces
of wartime took over. I used to buy soap and brilliantine from the
NAAFI and flog them to the KATCOMs, who split the soap into
smaller squares and the brilliantine into littler bottles to sell in
Seoul. The ladies there were desperate for toiletries and they
loved the smell of the brilliantine and used it as perfume, even
though it was really hair-oil and I don't know if they knew that
or not. The KATCOMs made a small fortune in their terms and
they gave me a cut of the profits.

There's always a bob or two to be had, ain't there – even in
the most hopeless of hinterlands.

After moving the military equipment, we were put to work
taking down defensive posts and dismantling living quarters.
These were mostly made up of sandbag walls, with one door in
and no way out and a flat roof covered in more sandbags. Now,
in Korea, there are about three million different kinds of snake
and two million nine hundred and ninety-nine thousand are poisonous. Every bag we took down, there was at least three or four
of the slitherers sliding about underneath and, to begin with, they
frightened the coloured faeces out of us and there'd be men lung-
ing and leaping about all over the place and shouting and
screaming. But, despite all the hullabaloo, I don't think anyone
ever got killed by a snake, at least not to my knowledge. Plenty
got bitten, mind you, but mostly by the non-deadly species. If
someone was unlucky enough to get struck by a poisonous
sidewinder, the medics had all sorts of anti-venom medicine
ready to treat them before they swelled up like a balloon and
floated off into the ozone.

But we got used to the snakes after a panicky period and got the job done in our own way. Once the roofs and doors were off, we just pushed the sandbag sides in and that was that. One day, a South Korean soldier caught this big tiger keelback and cut its head off. The thing was about five foot long and thick as a teenager's arm and it was wriggling like an eel in a knapsack. He grinned over at me and spoke in his Korean accent.

'For dinner . . . we have roast snake.'

Now, I didn't like the slimy-scaleys all that much as it was, but the thought of eating one of them nearly made me throw up. He cooked it in a three-foot-long shell case, propped up on two bits of rock with a fire underneath, and after about twenty minutes he took the thing out and cut it into slices and offered some to me. He was grinning with his whole gob and looking like Santy Claus opening his sack on Christmas Day and I didn't want to offend him – like I didn't want to offend the long-shirt who shoved me into the belly-dancing tent. All my mates were sitting around, waiting for me to taste the snake, and some of them were taking bets behind my back. So I took a small piece and looked at it closely to make sure it was dead. Then I turned to the South Korean.

'What about the poison?'

He stripped his teeth and pointed to them.

'Only in the fangs.'

I didn't know if this was true or not, but I took a bite all the same. It tasted like a cross between roast chucken and river-eel. Not too bad at all, so I ate the whole slice. He handed me another one.

'You like?'

'Nice . . . very nice.'

Now all the others wanted some too and it wasn't long before the whole snake was swallowed and not even the scales left.

The KATCOMs also got a weekly issue of desiccated octopus and, after eating the snake, I thought I'd try some of that too. This stuff looked like strips of leather and tasted like a horse's harness, but the more I chewed it, the more moist it got. Now, the KATCOMs told me to only take a small tiny nibble of it at a time, but I took a big bite and this thing in my mouth started to swell up like a sponge filling with water and it was growing too big to get back out of my gob and I was starting to choke. I was dancing up and down from one leg to the other, with people slapping me on the back and others trying to get their fingers into my mouth to prise out the swelling squid and I was starting to turn blue. Then two of the KATCOMs grabbed me and one of them held my mouth open and the other took out a small knife and shoved it in between my teeth and sliced the octopus in two and I thought the bugger must've taken my tongue away as well. Then he dragged half the tentacle from my mouth with his fingers and I was able to spit out the rest. For a while after that, I was called 'octo-puss'. Which I didn't like at all.

After we'd demolished all the little sandbag houses on the front line, I was approached by an officer called Captain Smith. He'd joined the army as a boy soldier and risen through the ranks over the twenty years he'd been in the service. A captain was the highest rank he could get to like this, without going to Sandhurst or some other royal college to become a Rupert. He ran a prison camp in Cairo during the war and, at reveille, the prisoners would all chuck their slop buckets at him. He punished them by giving them no food for a couple of days and they stopped when they got hungry enough and had no shit left to sling. But when they were fed for a while, they started throwing the slop buckets again and this went on the whole while he was there. Anyway, the captain was the only officer I ever had any time for and he heard I was an apprentice bricklayer in civvy street and asked me if I could build an officers' mess for him on the Kansas Line.

'I think so, sir.'

'Right, Sears, that's your next job then.'

I didn't have any bricks or blocks, so I used empty ammunition boxes instead. After laying a course of boxes, I opened the lids and filled them with sand and cement, then I locked down the lids and laid the next course. Because I had no way of cutting the metal boxes, I had to have the corners overhanging at each course up to plate high and I cut and shaped stones to keep each window opening upright. The Pioneer Corps dug up these great big rocks, which most of the hills were made out of, underneath, and I'd shape 'em out with a hammer and bolster, like a stone mason. I used Perspex from crashed aircraft as glass, so the officers could see out at us squaddies and laugh their chinless heads off. On the inside, I used eight-by-four sheets of plywood to cover the tin boxes and I painted the interior white. I even built a fireplace out of the chiselled stone at one end, to make it more homely. On the grand opening night, Captain Smith gave me and the lads who worked with me four crates of beer to celebrate with.

It was the first purpose-built officers' mess in Korea – and maybe the only one.

My next job was fuel storeman, issuing petrol to heat the tents and keep the cookhouse and the company vehicles going as well. The store was an open area with no camouflage or cover of any kind and if an enemy shell had ever come over and landed in the middle of it, we'd have been blown back to Blighty. All the petrol, or gasoline as the Yanks called it, was stored in forty-gallon drums and I'd have to order replacements on a regular basis. Some of the drums wouldn't be completely empty by the time they had to be taken away to be filled up again. There might be four or five gallons left inside, and I had to empty this residue into a pit filled with sand. The pit was twelve foot square and six foot deep and I must have emptied hundreds of gallons of gasoline away in my time as fuel storeman. It was the most ridiculous system I'd ever seen and, if only I had that reject fuel today, I'd be on the Forbes rich list.

After hostilities ended on 27 July, things got back to the regular army bullshit of square-bashing and parades and all that bluster. It started with having to do daily one-hour drills from 0830 hours to 0930 hours – marching in ranks of four and rifles at the ready and then back to the work we'd been doing since we got to Korea. I was down close to the cookhouse one day when I heard this loud scream. I looked up from whatever I was doing and saw a young South Korean soldier on fire and running blindly about like a mole in the moonlight. I grabbed a heavy blanket off a line and ran after him and rugby-tackled him to the ground. Then I smothered the fire with the blanket and managed to put out the flames. His arms and chest were burned to bits and the skin was hanging off him in cinder-strips. I found out later that a jerrycan of petrol got knocked over him by accident and ignited by the flames from the open oven. An army ambulance took him to the nearest field hospital, but he died there a couple of days later. The smell of his burning skin stayed in my nose and throat for a long time and sometimes I dream about it even now – so many long years later.

And the smell comes back to me.

Another morning I woke up sweating and wasn't able to get out of my angle-iron-and-brushwood bed. The orderly corporal called the medic who told me I had a mild dose of malaria. 'Malaria' is supposed to mean 'bad air', I think, but it was a bad mosquito that gave it to me and nothing much to do with the air at all. We all had to take three tablets every day before breakfast for prevention purposes or we got no breakfast, but it didn't stop me getting the bloody disease. I was sent to the hospital tent and had to stay there for nearly a week, which I didn't mind at all because I could swing the lead once the fever went away and I stopped seeing stuff like the Pink Elephants on Parade from the Disney film *Dumbo*. They treated me with penicillin injections, which cured everything in them days but nothing nowadays, and the MO told me when I was leaving that the malaria might come back every year for a while, but would only last for a few hours. And it did – every April for the next ten years I got bloody malaria again. It stayed around for a shorter and shorter time each year, until it disappeared altogether into the good air of England. I must've been the only man in Treacle Bumstead with malaria, because they had no treatment for it and all I could do was stay indoors until it was gone – otherwise they might have misdiagnosed my symptoms and banged me up in the loony bin like the Queen's cousins.

Then one night I was doing stag with my mate Dave Griffiths – who got sunburned on the *Asturias*, if you remember – when we saw this big wildcat that had been scavenging for food around the cookhouse for some time. We were told these Dokdo cats could be very dangerous, so I said to Dave, 'I'm gonna shoot the bugger!'

I put a round up the spout of my 303 and shot the cat straight through the head and killed it instantly. But the noise of the shot woke people up on half the hills around us and the next minute, we had officers swarming all about like bad-tempered bees.

'Sears, did you discharge your weapon?'

'Yes, sir.'

'Why?'

'That cat there . . . it was attacking us.'

'It's the colonel's pet tabby.'

Well, he must've been overfeeding it because it was as big as a bloody Labrador.

Next day, I was put on a charge for wasting ammunition. I had to fizz over to the command tent at 0900 hours to take whatever was coming to me but, luckily, it was Captain Smith, who I got along with alright, and he listened to my story.

'It was a big bugger and coming straight for us.'

'Bloody thing is always howling at night.'

'How was I to know, sir?'

'Where's the carcass?'

'Up on the ridge.'

'Charge dismissed.'

'What about the colonel?'

'We'll tell him the cat's missing in action.'

Captain Smith had the cat skinned and made a furry hat from its hide. No doubt the animal's bald carcass cooked up a nice *kimchi* for the KATCOMs as well – it was so fat it could've fed forty hungry South Koreans for a fortnight.

As I already said, I didn't much like the Yanks to begin with, but they started to grow on me after a while – mostly because I found I could make some easy money out of them. Our boots were better than theirs – they had an inner lining that kept your feet well warm in winter. Our army trousers were seven layers thick and lightweight with it and the Yanks took a shine to them along with our parkas. I got myself a job in the G1098 store after the petrol distribution job. The store supplied tactical equipment to the troops, and I used to sell the jackets and trousers to the Americans – three quid for a pair of boots and another three quid for trousers and three more quid for a parka – all in US dollars. You'll probably ask why nobody noticed this stuff going missing but, before the armistice, stock-taking was nonexistent and I could bamboozle the counts by putting the worn-out army-wear that came back up on the shelves as new. The Yanks dyed the stuff I sold them to their own shade of green, which was more brownish than our shade and nobody noticed. But I had to knock it on the head after the armistice, because they brought back all the bullshit and started checking everything properly. Still, it was a nice little number while it lasted.

The summer of 1953 was hot as the hob of hell. I'd been paddling my feet in a small stream on our hill to keep them cool sometimes and I thought, why not build a swimming pool? The hill was called Essex Hill and it had a number as well as a name, but I've forgotten what that was. It was Highland huge and a bit flat on top like a Helvellyn fell and there was plenty of room for a pool. I grabbed a pick, shovel and crowbar from the G1098 store and dyked up the stream and diverted it downhill into an unused paddy field. But the hill was mostly rock, under a thin layer of dry topsoil, and the job was too big for one man, so I had a word with Captain Smith and asked for help. The captain took a look and said I could have the help if the officers could have the pool for two hours a day. That seemed like a fair deal to me, so I agreed — as long as they used it between 1200 hours and 1500 hours, which was their off-duty time. That gave them three exclusive hours and then it would become a free-for-all. Before I could say 'swimming with staff officers', I had the services of four Royal Engineers and a compressor, and enough gun cotton to blow out the big Grand Coulee Dam. In two days, our pool was blasted out of the bare hillside, with a lining of rock that held the stream-water that flowed into it. It was thirty foot long by twenty foot wide by six foot deep and I christened it by having my first bath since arriving in Korea. Six of us stripped naked and jumped in and splashed about like a bunch of little brats.

But Captain Smith wanted a bigger ceremony.

'Right, Sears, here's what we'll do ...'

He organised a band and booze and I organised a smartly dressed rifle squad for a ceremonial guard. As well as beer for the boys, the captain also organised tables and chairs and sandwiches and spirits for the officers and we formed a guard of honour and the band struck up a jaunty rendition of 'St Patrick's Day in the Mornin' O' and we all had a party. We were eating and drinking and singing and the officers were getting tipsy at the table. Captain Smith had one more thing to do, he had a sign made up that said:

THIS POOL WAS DUG OUT BY
PRIVATE SOLDIERS OF
D COMPANY – ESSEX REGIMENT
FOR THE USE OF UN FORCES IN KOREA

We ran out of food and drink by about 1300 hours and the officers started taking off their clothes. Captain Smith turned to us squaddies.

'Right lads, off you go. The officers will look after this pool for the next two hours.'

Those of us who were off duty could come back at 1500 hours when the officers were finished and from then on it was open house on the hillside and anyone who wanted could come for a swim, as long as they didn't dog it. I turned back and shouted at the officers as they were getting ready to jump ball-swinging into the cold spring water.

'No pissing in the pool! That goes for the officers as well!'

Even the Americans came over and would dive off the backs

of their great big trucks and sometimes bang their heads on the rock-bottom. They loved having showers, the Yanks, so I got the idea to channel some of the stream away with angle iron into biscuit tins with holes in them that made lovely cold sprinklers and some of it could be siphoned off for pure drinking water as well. The residue drained down into the paddy field and helped bring the dry slopes back to life, so everybody was happy.

I had plenty of customers from other companies as well as the Yanks for the spring water, because the regular drinking stuff came from the River Imjin and tasted like it'd seeped through a sumpful of stinking squaddie-boots. It was brown and brought up from the river in bowsers and strained through canvas sacking with water-purifying tablets. It had to be left settling for twenty-four hours, but it still looked like it came out of an alcoholic's arse after a spicy vindaloo and you had to close your eyes when you drank it. So my little dammed-up stream became very popular. The Yanks traded smokes and cookies and Hershey bars and a chocolate drink in a can with a ring at the bottom – when you pulled the ring, the drink heated up and they called it a 'hot toddy'. I was happy to barter because the American K rations were far superior to our hardtack – they had steak and fruit and other tasty tuck.

We had nothing like that at all.

12

The Golden Ginza Club

After three months in Korea, I got my first leave – ten days in Tokyo. Seoul Airport was being run by the Americans and us R&R people were driven down there in three-tonners. We boarded a US four-engined Stratocruiser transport plane with wooden slats for seats that took four arse-numbing hours to fly to Haneda Airport. It was noisy with no insulation and we huddled up against the bare hull, forty or fifty men along each side. There was all kinds in that old crate – Americans and Brits and Aussies and Canadians and New Zealanders, all saying nothing and pretending not to worry about one of the wings falling off. Once we safely landed, more trucks took us to our 'hotel', which was called the Kookaburra Club, about three miles outside the city. Well, this place was as big as a bailiwick – it had tennis courts and cricket pitches and swimming pools and cinemas and everything a soldier could want – except strumpets.

The Yanks had their own hacienda, separate from the rest of

us, and there were different areas inside the Kookaburra Club for British troops and Australian troops and Canadian troops and New Zealand troops and we were billeted in large dormitories, four storeys high. The place was staffed by Japanese cleaners who came in to the dorms and cleaned them up and changed the sheets and it was a bit like being back with the nuns in the Black Forest – but not as cerebral. The eating area was football-field sized and the grub was nearly as good as the stuff I was getting from the Yanks and we could book out at the guardroom and not have to book back in again for the full ten days, if we didn't want to – or else just come back to kip if things got a bit too raucous. Which they did once or twice. Like I said, the Kookaburra Club had almost everything and you didn't need to go outside if you didn't have a yearning to. I had about fifteen quid in sterling and another 200 dollars I made from selling clothes to the Yanks and hair-oil to the hookers of Seoul.

Anyway, I decided to book myself out for the full ten days and have the whole lot together. I took fifty packs of condoms with me that had three Frenchies in each pack – I was probably being optimistic, but this was my first time in Tokyo and I wanted to be well prepared. After the piano player at the Hole in the Wall I was no novice when it came to sexual intercourse any more and I palled up with this Australian called Wally, who supplied me with a load of penicillin tablets, which were supposed to stop you from catching any kind of clap. The Aussies got them as standard issue, but we didn't. Maybe it was something to do with all the goats in Aden, or because the Aussies were more susceptible to VD than us Brits – who knew?

Before leaving the guardroom, we were told not to frequent the small drinking bars outside the Kookaburra complex, as these were considered to be bad for your general health. So as soon as we got outside, we went into the first one we came to. I went up to the small serving hatch and this middle-aged Japanese woman dressed in a kimono told me, in Yum-Yum English, to sit down and she'd come and take our order. There was four of us and, as soon as we sat down, four Japanese girls came gushing out from somewhere and sat on our laps. They were young and sexy and dressed in side-split skirts and it was clear they weren't going nowhere until they cajoled some hard currency out of us. When the mama-san came back with our beers, we asked her how much for just a short session. Because we had other places to go – people to see.

'One hundred yen.'

That was about two shillings sterling and seemed like a bargain to me. We had two goes apiece over the course of the next hour and then caught a cab into central Tokyo.

Everybody drove on the right in Tokyo City because it was controlled by the Americans after the war and they'd only be confused if people drove on the left like they did in the rest of the country. We were dropped in Ginza Street, which was the equivalent of Soho in London, only Soho never looked anything like this! There were clubs and bars all in a row like tarts teasing and the biggest and brightest was the Golden Ginza Club – so in we went. The Golden Ginza Club was kitted out like a pasha's palace: the finest furnishings and topless girls sliding around a thin metal post long before the West discovered this form of entertainment. More topless waitresses served drinks and all sorts of people were out on the floor dancing. A band up on the low stage played the latest hits and we sat down to enjoy the ambience. We drank until after midnight and then arranged for four of the pole-dancers to accompany us to the nearest hotel. These girls were half-Korean and half-Japanese, the legacy of the comfort women who were provided for the Nipponese soldiers when they occupied Korea during the war.

A full night at the hotel, including the girls and a communal bath, cost twelve dollars and I paid for it all out of my sideline profits. The beds were flat on the floor and the place was so cheap the small rooms were only separated by thin paper walls – so everyone could hear what everyone else was doing. In the early hours of the morning, the Aussie next to me let out a loud scream and his Japanese consort came flying though the paper partition and on to my bed – sporting an eye that was already beginning to bruise.

'She bit my cock!'

'For Christ's sake.'

'So I belted the bitch!'

The commotion attracted the attention of the hotel management and they called for the American Military Police who patrolled the area in case of any trouble from UN troops. We'd heard that these guys were particularly brutal when it came to dishing out their own justice, so we made a dash for the door. The hullabaloo spooked the rest of the hotel's clients, who also decided it wasn't the healthiest place to be and followed us fast to the exit. Now, it's the custom in Japan that all footwear should remain at the entrance of their ryokans and there must have been at least fifty of us tear-arseing round looking for boots and shoes and brothel-creepers and clogs and the confusion was like bath night in bedlam. In the end, we just slipped our feet into whatever was a close enough size and legged it down the street and grabbed a taxi back to the Kookaburra Club until the fuss died down.

Next day, after breakfast, we decided it might be safe to go back into the city. The Aussie said the girl was giving him a hum-job when she accidentally bit his dick and we asked him to show us his schlong to see what damage she'd done.

'Jesus, you'd better go see the doc, Aus.'

'Why's that, Ken?'

'Her teeth broke the skin and it's all blue and 'orrible.'

'You're kidding!'

'Might be gangrene.'

'Strewth!'

'Might even fall off.'

Next thing, the Aussie was gone at full speed to see the medics. We laughed when he left, because it wasn't all that bad, but he deserved it for causing us all that grief the night before – and for belting the young karayuki-san. We carried on to one of the small bars outside the Kookaburra complex and waited for him to catch up with us. He was relieved his wang wasn't gonna wither and fall off and took the joke in good form. From there we went back into the Golden Ginza Club and had a meal and got stuck back into the booze again. We danced the cha-cha with the club girls and every dance cost about 2½d in the real money of the day, which would be about one penny now.

Later on, trouble erupted again when a black American soldier punched one of the dancing girls. He was either drunk or high on something and was way out of his head. There was a huge commotion and the Yankee MPs came and dragged this guy out and beat him unconscious with their batons and then slung him into the back of an open truck and took him away. Thing about it was, the Yank redcaps treated us Brits exactly the same as their own men and some of them carried baseball bats – we were glad they didn't get hold of us the night before. They could hold you in their cells before turning you over to the Brit guardhouse and if they held you for twenty-one days you'd be AWOL and put on a charge. But if they held you for twenty-two days – and they could – you were classed as a deserter and court-martialled. That meant a year or two in a tough glass-house, either the French-Canadians in Seoul or some other shithole in Japan. So, there were never any rucks in the Golden Ginza Club and we never had any trouble with the Yanks or anyone else. They didn't have bouncers or doormen because they didn't need 'em. The Yank redcaps were enough to deter any violence.

The rest of my stay in Tokyo carried on more or less in the same vein – booze and debauchery and bawdy singing. Not exactly wine, women and song – more beer and Japanese abazures[13] and drunken army-shanties. I won't bore you with the details, except to mention my mate Harry from Leighton Buzzard. Harry was still a virgin and the girls knew this because

13 Prostitutes.

he didn't know what to do with them, and when he found out he came his coco in his underpants before he could even get it in. But, according to *yūkaku* custom, this extended celibacy entitled him to a Golden Ginza Club girl free of charge for the rest of the week. Apparently, it was an honour for a Japanese girl to deflower a man – I don't know if it still is, or if that man had to be non-Japanese. If I'd known the rules, I'd have made out I was a virgin too. I also got a taste for saki, the Japanese fermented rice drink. What we'd do was to buy a bottle of whisky in the shops, which was cheaper than beer, and bring it into the clubs with us and mix it with the saki. It was a cheap cocktail and a good way of getting drunk, and you didn't go blind on it.

But I forgot to tell you about that – the time I went blind from drinking *makkoli*, or Korean homemade moonshine. The KATCOMs used to bring this stuff back with them from Seoul and it was a kind of milky-white distillation and I didn't know whether to eat it or drink it because it was like a cross between soup and yoghurt. Some of them called it *nongju*, which translated roughly as hillbilly drink. Anyway, a few of us were off duty on this weekend when the KATCOMs came back with a few bottles of *makkoli* and it seemed like a good idea to try it. I was up for drinking anything at the time, as long as it had alcohol in it, and it didn't taste too bad because we were already on the beer and our taste buds were banjaxed. So we did the lot and had a good time with the Koreans, singing and dancing round the hills and hollows and we were pretty pissed when we finally got to bed.

Next morning, when I woke up, I couldn't see a thing and at

first I thought it was a dream and I wasn't really awake. But slowly it dawned on me I *was* awake and I was also blind. So I started to shout out for someone to come and help me and I could hear other men shouting out the same thing. I managed to climb out of my sleeping bag and started to feel my way round the tent and I could hear others falling over things and I knew they were just as blind as me. We thought the North Koreans or the Chinese must've dropped some kind of gas on us or another such chemical weapon and we were panicking and banging round and bumping into each other and calling for the medics.

'Get back into your bloody bunks!'

It was the duty sergeant's voice and we did what he said. Whether or not we were in our own bunks or somebody else's, we didn't know nor care.

'It's the hooch.'

'Sorry, Sarg?'

'It's the Korean rotgut, it sends you blind.'

'Jesus Christ!'

'Don't worry, it's not permanent. It'll wear off in a few hours.'

And it did. We just lay on the sleeping bags until our sight came back and I swore I'd never drink anything I couldn't see through again.

On our last evening in the Kookaburra Club, we played bingo for a rollover pot of £105 – which was a lot of money. I was sitting with a lad called Jock Gibson and I needed one number to win it.

'If this comes up, Jock, me and you will go AWOL.'

'I'm with you, Ken.'

But someone else called 'house' before they pulled my number and it wouldn't have mattered anyway, because the geezer didn't get the cash in his hand – it was transferred to his army savings account. They probably knew full well if they gave a soldier that sum of money in Tokyo, they wouldn't see him again for a long while.

They certainly wouldn't have seen me.

Next morning, after breakfast, we boarded the trucks to take us back to the American airbase. After about an hour into the flight, we noticed oil spraying out of one of the engines and covering the windows. After the pilot was informed, we were issued with Mae Wests (inflatable lifejackets). But there was one short and this young Yank started panicking and he was doing my swede in with his bloody hysterics.

'Here, take mine, you big babby!'

'Can I, sir?'

'Sure. If we hit the water from this height, you'll be wearing your arsehole for a monocle.'

I don't think he knew what a monocle was. But the pilot turned the crate round and took us back to base in Tokyo. The young soldier looked a bit sheepish when we disembarked and tried to make out he wasn't really worried.

As a reward for being so brave, we were taken over to the cookhouse at the American base near the Kookaburra Club and treated to a proper slap-jack meal. I chose steak and the piece of meat filled the whole plate. The veg was cooked in sugar instead of salt and this was a bit alien to my Treacle Bumstead taste buds and took some swallowing, and they gave us things called French fries, which tasted like English chips to me and I didn't know whether I should sprinkle sweat or salt'n'vinegar on them. But that steak was the best I've ever eaten – before or since. For afters we had blueberry pie and custard, cooked without sugar, and I was sure the Yanks got their ingredients mixed up and put the sugar in the veg instead of the pie by mistake. I wouldn't put it past them.

It took three hours to fix the transport plane and we boarded it a second time and took off again for Korea. But the same thing happened and it stared leaking oil all over the place and the pilot turned it round again and took us back to Tokyo. It was getting a bit late at night by now and they gave us a small supper without any steak and a blanket and pillow and told us to doss down on the reception floor. We were woken at 0500 hours and told to wash and shave and then sat down for a big American breakfast of pancakes and bacon and waffles and coffee and anything else we could cram down our gullets.

Boy, oh boy, was that grub better than ours!

We boarded the transport plane for the third time and the pilot told us a new engine had been fitted and that filled us with confidence. I looked over at the young cry-babby and I could see he was still fretting about falling into the Sea of Japan – and I wondered how he'd cope in a real crisis. But the Stratocruiser held together and the pilot got us safely back to Seoul this time. That trip to Tokyo and back was my first flying experience and I swore I'd never get on a plane ever again – and I never have. But then, maybe it was worth it for the feed?

Not long afterwards, me and another private were detailed, along with a sergeant, to take a British prisoner from another company to the notorious UN prison in Seoul. The man was sentenced to 105 days for being caught out of bounds on night-time stag duty. The nick was run by the Princess Patricia's Canadian Light Infantry – the PPCLI – and it was rumoured that a man was beaten to death there every month. They could and would fabricate reports if you died from the brutality and harsh treatment and it would be covered up by everyone because of it being a war situation. The prison colonel-in-chief wouldn't go against his own men, otherwise there'd be anarchy and the prisoners would be throwing their slop buckets at him like they did at Captain Smith in Algiers. Like in every society, some people deserved to be in jail because they weren't happy otherwise, but others didn't need to be in that place, just for some trivial offence that annoyed a petty NCO. But they were put there by the bastards who took jobs as military police and corporals and glasshouse guards. They thrived in them jobs and weren't fit to be out in the regular regiments.

Later on, the 1965 film *The Hill*, starring Sean Connery and Harry Andrews, was based on this French-Canadian prison in Seoul, even though its identity was never given away in the film. And conditions were just as bad, if not worse, than what was shown in the movie.

After we arrived, we helped the prisoner carry his belongings to the main gate. When it opened, this big French-Canadian corporal started screaming at us to drop the prisoner's kit and make the man carry it all himself. Although our sergeant outranked the *bouchard*,[14] we were out of our jurisdiction and he knew it. He told the sergeant he was placing us all on a charge and roared at us to double-quick march across to the guardroom. Double-quick march is almost running and the guardroom was about a hundred yards away and all the prisoner's stuff was falling out and scattered all over the square-yard. In the guardroom, we were shouted to attention by the big French-Canadian and bollocked by an even more arrogant officer for our sloppy behaviour and there was nothing any of us could do about it. If we'd given back any lip, we'd have been arrested immediately and be joining the unfortunate soldier doing the 105 days.

When we got back to base, I asked the sergeant if we were really on a charge. He said, when we were at the glasshouse, we were automatically under French-Canadian jurisdiction and they could do what they wanted. But once they let us leave, their jurisdiction ended and we could forget about any charges being brought. I thought to myself, thank the Lord and his mate Lucifer for that. I remembered all the strokes I'd pulled and was glad I'd never ended up in a stink-hole like that. Little did I know how close I would come to going back there on the sinful side of the handcuffs not long after.

14 Bigmouth.

13

Marilyn and Me

By now it was coming up to Christmas 1953 and there wasn't much to cheer up the dull, demilitarised winter days. I wanted to be at home, tucked up in the nice temperate climate of Hertfordshire instead of being out there in the bitter twenty-below temperature and the three-inch ice crystals on the marquee in the morning and the knee-deep snow and the ball-biting winds. And none of the nonsense stopped for these bone-chilling conditions. Everything went on as usual – the drilling and the early-morning parades and the night-time stag and all the rest of the bullshit and blustering. But not much in the way of anything else – no sports or boxing or football or running. Just work during the day and guard duty during the perishing nights. We did have a film show once a week, outside on the hill in the evening. We'd have layers of clothes on and still be sitting there freezing to the metal-framed folding chairs. The American Cinema Unit supplied the films and I remember one in particular called *Gentlemen Prefer Blondes*, starring Jane Russell and Marilyn Monroe, and I thought to myself, what a stunner that Marilyn is. What I wouldn't give to meet her on a moonlit night.

Some weekends the Aussies and Kiwis would come over because their NAAFI tent stopped serving beer at 1800 hours and ours kept it going till 2200 hours. As they got paid twice the money we did, they were more than happy to pay for our drinks as well as their own. We were only allowed bottled beer on our line, in case we wouldn't be able to get up in the mornings, but they brought their Hogs bourbon and Feeney's Irish and guitars and banjos and harmonicas with them and we'd sit around sometimes and have a sing-song till the early hours. I loved it.

The marquees were heated by chuffa stoves during the cold winter and they ran on petrol fed from outside through a rubber pipeline with a figure-of-eight loop to stop any blowback from the stove itself. But some idiots left them on all the time if the weather got really down below freezing and, if the loop wasn't secure enough, it only took a couple of minutes for the stack pipe to get red hot. The residue collected under the stoves and, if they weren't tended to, this stuff caught fire and then the stove went up. If the stove went up, the marquee went up too, with very little time to get out – maybe two minutes. You'd be on your own hill and then you'd see a sudden burst of fire on some other hill when a marquee caught light, and men galloping out of them and scattering everywhere – running round like little spiders in the distance. It never happened on our hill and I never heard of anyone being killed, but I'm sure some got burned bad.

Like I said, it was coming up to my second Christmas in the

army and we weren't allowed to buy spirits of any kind in the
'Ship Inn', just beer. The Ship Inn was a prefab pub the Royal
Engineers built after the armistice and it was shared by all the regiments, and maybe they thought it was unchristian-like to drink
whisky at Christmas. Now, I didn't drink spirits all that much
myself, except for the saki and the home-brew that made me go
blind, but a lot of others liked a drop of the hard stuff at Yuletide,
so I got in touch with a couple of Yanks who used to buy the
clothes from me when I was in the G1098 store and arranged to
do a deal, exchanging bottles of our strong beer for their bottles
of spirits – mostly Southern Comfort and gin and rum. The
exchange rate was four bottles of beer for one bottle of spirit and,
don't forget, the beer was in large half-litre bottles. I swapped
three crates of beer, with twenty-four bottles in each, for eighteen bottles of spirits. I also swapped an extra crate for a box of
fifty cigars and what the Americans called cookies – biscuits to me
and you. They gave us King Edwards soaked in rum because they
considered them to be inferior cigars – they liked the Cubans
better, even if they didn't like Fidel Castro all that much.

On Christmas day, I invited some soldiers from other companies to join us and bring what they had and we accumulated
enough for a proper Christmas dinner, with turkey and pork and
cranberry sauce and Christmas pud and custard. Then we built
a big fire and sat round it drinking the beer and spirits and eating
the cookies and smoking the cigars and singing, well into the
early hours of Boxing Day. The officers left us alone because they
didn't want to be on duty either and nobody even noticed that it
was minus twenty-two degrees in the carol-singing coldness.

Then, in February 1954, I found myself doing guard duty on the road from Seoul to the Kansas Line. Anyway, this one night on stag with Dave Griffiths, I noticed a cortège of about five limousines coming towards us, led by an American Jeep. There was a two-tonner at the rear with a guard detail of Yankee troops, so I knew it must've been someone special. I moved into the centre of the road and held up my hand to stop the procession from proceeding. They halted and I shouted out the first part of the password:

'High!'

The American officer in the Jeep shouted back:

'Hi, fella.'

The password was 'high noon'. I put my rifle up to my shoulder.

'Wrong password.'

'Sorry, son, I don't know it.'

'Then you're going nowhere.'

The Yank officer started to laugh and this riled me a bit.

'Hey, boy, we have Marilyn Monroe and Joe DiMaggio in the third car down.'

'You're still going nowhere, unless you know the password.'

The officer stopped laughing and his face got a bit florid.

'You can't hold us up here!'

'Sure I can.'

The American climbed down out of his Jeep and put his hands in the air when I aimed the rifle at his head.

'Listen, fella, let's sort this out.'

'How?'

'Come with me.'

He led me down along the line of cars until we came to a big Cadillac, while Dave kept them covered. I looked in the window and, true enough, there was Marilyn Monroe sitting on the back seat in the moonlight, along with some geezer who looked a bit like George Formby only bigger and brown-tanned. She was the most beautiful woman I ever saw and my chin melted and fell down as far as my belt. She slid across to the window and rolled it down and my heart skipped several beats.

'Kirk?'

'Ken, miss.'

'Oh, sorry . . . why don't you come see the show, soldier.'

I tried to say, 'Thanks, I'd love to,' but my mouth wasn't working, probably because of my chin being on my chest, and nothing came out – except for 'high noon'. The American officer clapped me on the back and said 'thanks' for me and the window rolled up again. Now that he knew the password, I had to let the convoy pass.

Marilyn and DiMaggio had just got married and were on a trip to Japan. She decided to take a detour to Korea to entertain the American troops and she performed ten shows in four days in front of 100,000 soldiers – but I wasn't one of them. I was put on a charge for letting the convoy pass without knowing the password. But some strings must've been pulled, because the charge got dropped and nothing more was said about it. Apart from me not being allowed over to the American sector to see the show, even though I was invited personally by Marilyn Monroe herself!

It got dark quick in Korea – it could be bright when you went over a hill on patrol at 1800 hours and then dark five minutes later – and it could take a soldier by surprise. A day or two later and I was asleep in the marquee when I felt this hand shaking me by the shoulder. I woke up and saw the Yank officer who was leading the convoy I stopped. He had a finger up to his lips and said, 'Sshhh!'

'What . . .?'

'Get dressed. Come with me.'

I wasn't sure what to do, but then I caught a glimpse of Captain Smith standing just outside the tent and he nodded his head. I got up and pulled my uniform on and the Yank took me over to a Jeep and we drove the four miles or so to the American sector.

He took me into a small private tent, well away from the main camp, that looked like it was a kind of dressing room, with a guard outside and Marilyn Monroe inside. It was bitter cold and she was dressed in a bomber jacket and trousers and a black high-necked sweater and huddled round a heater. But she still looked beautiful. Joe DiMaggio was sitting on a chair behind her. He spoke first.

'We're heading back to the States, but my wife wanted to see you.'

Marilyn came over and took a closer look at me.

'I thought you were Kirk.'

I found my voice.

'Kirk?'

'Douglas. When you came to the Caddy. I said, "What's Kirk

doing here, are they making a movie?" But they told me you weren't Kirk and I wanted to see for myself.'

'I'm Ken ... not Kirk.'

'I know.'

I stammered.

'They ... er, they wouldn't ... they wouldn't let me come see the ... the show.'

'Oh no, what a shame. We gotta give Ken something, Joe. They wouldn't let him come see the show.'

DiMaggio just shrugged his shoulders like he didn't care much, even if I had been Kirk Douglas, and Marilyn looked round the tent, but there wasn't much in there. The Yank officer had me by the arm by now and was leading me back outside.

'Here ...'

Marilyn picked up a perfume bottle and kissed me on the cheek when she handed it to me and I thanked her and put it in my pocket.

Before I knew it, I was back in my sleeping bag and, next morning, I couldn't believe what happened wasn't a dream. Then I found the perfume bottle. I sprayed it to see if it was brilliantine hair-oil, but it wasn't – it was proper eau-de-femme-fatale. That was sixty years ago and the perfume bottle has stayed with me all that time. It got kicked around in my kitbag in Korea and the perfume all evaporated, but the bottle's still there. And I don't care if people believe this story or not – I know it happened and that's all that matters to me. When Marilyn Monroe died in 1962 I was devastated. To me, she was the most wonderful woman I ever met – apart from the woman I married.

Ever since my twentieth birthday on 21 January 1954, I was counting the days until I got demobbed. And sure enough, my name came up with all the others on Battalion Orders. I was to hand in my rifle and all the other gear belonging to the G1098 stores the day before I was due to leave Korea. But on the day of handing everything in, an amendment was made to Battalion Orders and I read it with dismay.

Private Sears K. – Number 22662012
Taken off this draft and will finish the time
he has spent in the guardhouse
3 months
He will leave on the next draft for England

I was to spend a full year in Korea because I had to do that extra three months for all the time I'd been banged up during my stint in the army. I went inside for two weeks in my very first month, then there was the twenty-eight days aboard ship – and a few other times as well. It came to three months altogether in bits and pieces and I had to serve it all out in Korea. I'll never forget that day, waving goodbye to all my mates who'd joined up with me and them laughing and shouting at me:

'Soldier on, Ken, you wanker!'

I shook my fist at them and shouted back:

'I'll get you bastards when I get back to Treacle Bumstead!'

And it served the buggers right when the troopship *Windrush*, which they were on, sank off the coast of North Africa. I was worried when I first heard the news, hoping they were alright and didn't drown. Apparently, an engine-room fire was caused when soot from the funnel fractured a fuel-supply pipe. An explosion and fierce oil fire killed four of the engine-room crew and couldn't be put out because the generators that worked the pumps were knackered. No power meant many of the lifeboats couldn't be launched and the ones that were couldn't hold all the passengers who were all in their shorts and night skivvies. Rescue vessels picked them up and took them to Algiers, where they were looked after by the French Army. I laughed my boots off and stood barefoot, after I found out all my mates survived. Teach them to take the Michael out of me!

Anyway, the weeks wore on and about five days before I was finally due to leave Korea, I was on night guard duty again and the corporal asked me to go over to the cookhouse and rustle up a few sausage sandwiches. Now, the cookhouse was off limits when it was closed and it was a serious offence for anyone to be found in there stealing stuff – especially me, stealth-fingered Sears. I had a look round the hill to make sure no nosy officer was snooping about, then slipped into the cookhouse and lit up the stove. I was just about to throw the sausages onto the spitting pan when a Second Lewy orderly officer came up behind me and nearly made me jump out of my jocks.

'What are you doing, soldier?'

'Er, I'm putting out the stove, sir.'

He got smart.

'Putting out the stove? You put out the cat, soldier, not the stove. But, then, you did, didn't you!'

Obviously a reference to the Fat Cat's fat-cat. He had it in for me.

'Corporal of the guard told me to check, sir.'

'Check what, soldier?'

I was trying to think on my feet and hoping he wouldn't see the sausages.

'Just in case anything was amiss, sir.'

'What's amiss is you, soldier. You're on a charge.'

He took my name and number and rank and I thought to myself, bloody hell, Ken, you're never gonna get out of the army at this rate!

As soon as the officer left to confirm my story with the corporal, I shot out the other end of the cookhouse and got to the guard tent first and dragged the corporal out under the flaps so I could fill him in and he wouldn't make a liar out of me – as well as a light-finger. I finished my stag that night and, when I went back to the guard tent, the corporal told me the officer was putting me on a charge anyway, even though he'd confirmed my story. I knew if I was found guilty it would be 110 days in the French-Canadian glasshouse in Seoul and, with my aversion to any kind of discipline, I'd be the next monthly statistic to be beaten to death there. I tried to decide whether I should do a runner, or take my chances on being found not guilty. It all depended on the officer in charge of the hearing. If I got a ramrod, I'd be goose-cooked for sure.

At 0100 hours the next morning, I was marched into the Ruperts' telling-off tent under escort. I was chopping straws with my arse until I saw who the orderly officer was – my old mate,

Captain Smith. I could've run over there and hugged the ugly bugger! My bumhole went back to its proper position and when the charge was read out, I was sure I saw a smile cross his face for a split second.

'Do I know you, soldier?'

'No, sir.'

'Are you sure?'

'Yes, sir.'

After hearing the corporal of the guard's evidence, Smith smiled again.

'You're a very lucky man, soldier.'

Because the corporal of the guard backed up my story, he said he had no alternative but to dismiss the charge. The blood came rushing back into my rectum and I let out the mother-and-sister of all sighs. On the way out, the Second Lewy scowled at me.

'You lucky bastard, how did you get out of that?'

'Just told the truth, sir.'

A few days later, it was my turn to leave Korea. I didn't think I'd ever make it. As I climbed into the back of the lorry, my mate Jock Gibson turned to me.

'Once we leave Pusan Harbour, Ken, we'll know we're on our way home.'

'And when we get to Japan, the first night's drinks are on me, Jock.'

We were sailing to Kure, a base in Hiroshima prefecture, on a small troopship. The trip took two days and the crossing from Korea to Japan wasn't too bad, apart from being boring. After disembarking, we marched to the transit camp, where we were to stay for ten days, till the ship that was to take us back to England arrived. It was like in Wuppertal when we were stationed in the SS quarters – this place was home to the Imperial Guard during the war and was a big step up from the fire-hazard marquees in Korea. The other good thing was, we were allowed to go into town whenever we liked, as long as we properly booked out and back in again.

The shipping port of Kure was a smaller version of Tokyo, geared up to making money from squaddies and matelots and all sorts of marine misfits. Jock and me headed straight for the nearest bar, which was called the Merry Garden – I still have a card advertising that place in my wallet to this very day. Like in all the harbour towns in Japan, these bars had mama-sans and young women for sale at low prices and us soldiers took advantage of that at the time. Whether it's something to be proud or ashamed of is a matter of personal conscience, but I didn't think much along them lines back then when I was but twenty summers upon the planet. The girls needed what we had, money – and we needed what they had. The way of the world since time began, I think.

The following day, me and Jock hired a couple of Suzuki two-stroke motorcycles and rode out into the countryside to see the sights. Even though we were in the province of Hiroshima, the country around Kure was full of fruit trees and apple-blossom and sparkling paddy and crops growing in terraces high up into the hills and low down to the inland sea. We found this traditional drinking place called an *izakay* that served Asahi lager and food as well and it was a kind of working-class bar for the Japanese.

The place was a lot different from the harbour clubs, full of friendly people and no *baishunfu* girls. We sat in the garden and this lady and her young daughter started talking to us. The older woman could speak a kind of pidjin English she picked up from the Yanks and the younger one was being taught English in school as a second language. The mother said her eldest daughter had married a Tommy who used to work in the transit camp we were staying at. They met a year before he got demobbed and he took her back with him to England. The lady asked me if I knew where Romford was and I told her it was in northeast London, which was the capital city of England – just like Tokyo in Japan. She said her daughter wrote to her every week and I advised her to save up some money and go see them. She'd already started, but it was hard for her, because she lost her husband in the war. She asked if England was nice and I told her it was – otherwise we wouldn't want to go back there. I wished them well and me and Jock left and I often wondered if she ever made it to Romford to visit her eldest daughter. And if she thought England was a nice place when she got there.

Two nights before leaving, Jock and me were in the Merry Garden and living up to the name of the place and due to book back into the transit camp that night. As it was so close to leaving-for-ever time and we knew we wouldn't be back here again, we decided to get a couple of girls and stay a bit longer – for a final fling. And that's what we did. But a bit longer turned into all night, and when we got back to camp we were immediately arrested and brought before the camp commander on a charge of being AWOL. We tried the old trick of saying we got back in time, but there was nobody in the guardroom to book us in – but this time they wouldn't wear it. We were fined a month's pay by Royal Warrant and confined to camp until our ship sailed. Now, a Royal Warrant fine meant 'double' in British Army language, so we were actually fined two months' pay. It seemed like an expensive fling, but we didn't give a toss and I was up for doing it again. And so was Jock. Apart from the fine, being AWOL just carried a sentence of jankers and we were practically on the troopship home, so what could they do to us? That night, we put our kitbags in our beds and covered them up to make out we were sleeping. Normally at lights out, the orderly corporal only checked to see if the beds were occupied and didn't bother to see what they were occupied with. Jock and me left by the back way and went out for the night.

When we got back at 0400 hours, we found the sergeant of the guard waiting for us – they'd only gone and done a routine check on the beds on the one night we went over the wall. Sod's law!

'You two prats have gone and done it now!'

'Sorry, Sarg.'

'You will be. You won't be going home.'

'Why not?'

'The ship sails at 1000 hours this morning and you'll be in front of the same officer as yesterday. He'll throw the bloody book at you.'

The sergeant was right. But the officer looked as if he'd been drinking jambava juice half the night and he didn't recognise us. He asked the orderly to bring in our records but, luckily for us, all the records were already on board the troopship *Devonshire*.

So we received the same punishment as the day before – a month's pay by Royal Warrant and confined to camp till the ship sailed. But, as the ship was sailing that morning, we didn't give a monkey's maiden-aunt. And when I finally got my demob money after being back in Treacle Bumstead for a while, I found that the Royal Warrant fines were never stopped.

What a result!

We left Japan that day on the troopship, heading for Hong Kong.

14

A Right Old Riot on the *Devonshire*

If we thought the *Asturias* was slow coming out, it was a super-powered speedboat compared to the *Devonshire*. With a top speed of only twelve knots, the old saltbucket was definitely a slow-boat from China. When we arrived at Kowloon Harbour after sailing for six days and six nights, we were given eight hours' shore leave. Most of the men stayed close to the ship and visited gift shops for presents to bring home to wives and mothers and babbas and brasses. I bought a camera for myself and a few china figures for my old lady that got half-inched from out of my kitbag while I was dozing on board the *Devonshire*. Ironically, the battered, dehydrating perfume bottle Marilyn gave me wasn't of any worth to the thieves and they left it where it was. I also picked up the same two books I bought on the way out – *A Night in a Moorish Harem* and *The Autobiography of a Flea*. I loaned these out at the same price as before, but with an extra shilling deposit that was refundable on return of the book. That way, I earned more money and the books lasted longer. I don't know what happened to them in the end, they probably got so worn out and dick-eared that I just threw them away or left them aboard the *Devonshire*.

On the way to Singapore, the dirty thieves struck again. This time they nicked my boots and cap. I think I told you already, if you lost any army gear, not only did you have to pay to have it replaced, but you had to pay for the stuff you lost too – double bubble! The cap cost 17s/6d and the boots cost £1/7s/6d – double that up and I'd lost a total of £5/10s, which pissed me off a bit to say the least. When I went up on deck the next morning, I saw this soldier from the Lancashire Royals (the Loyals) wearing what I had reason to believe was my cap. I knew it was an Essex Regiment cap because ours had a purple diamond behind the hat-badge – this was awarded for a famous regimental victory against Napoleon at the battle of Salamanca in 1812, where the 44th Foot (which later became part of the Essex Regiment) captured the eagle standard of a French regiment, a great honour at the time. Anyway, I looked down at this soldier's boots and recognised them as mine too from the scuffmarks. That was enough for me, without saying a word, I laid into him and gave him a bloody good up-and-down-the-deck and took the cap and boots back. But my assault on the thief turned into a riot – the Essex lads against the Loyals, it was like a scene out of a Western, with blokes flying through windows and doors and smashing each other across the yuds with chairs and the officers and NCOs tearing their hair out trying to stop it. We all got arrested, of course, and were stood in front of the CO with black eyes and bitten ears and flattened noses and tufts of hair missing from the sides of heads and it fell to me to explain what it was all about, seeing as I'd started it. I didn't want to grass nobody, but what else could I do? That launched a search of the Loyals' quarters and a lot of the missing gear was found there – but not my mother's china figures. The Loyals were given extra duties and fined for their thieving misdemeanours, but there was nothing much more the brass could do to them. I mean, they couldn't make them paint coal or weed thistles aboard ship, could they?

It took another nine days to get to Singapore and by the time we docked things had settled back down on board the *Devonshire*. We were given another eight hours' shore leave and by this time I was overdue for demob, so I asked one of the officers if I was still under army regulations.

'Not if you don't want to be, Sears, it's up to you.'

'Lovely jubbly!'

'But you'll have to leave the ship and find your own way home.'

I had second thoughts about that one and came to the conclusion I'd be better off to stay as I was till we landed back in Blighty. So I went ashore and bought some more china figures and then got pissed, as per usual practice.

From Singapore, we sailed to Colombo in Ceylon and we crossed the equator at night on the way back, so I didn't see any celebrations like the pool-ducking and the nose-scouring on the way out. We arrived in Colombo at the same time as Queen Elizabeth II, who was on a Commonwealth tour. The Royal

Yacht *Britannia* was docked in the harbour and I went ashore and saw her and the Duke of Edinburgh waving from their open-backed Rolls-Royce as they drove down Main Street. There was a huge crowd gathered, all waving flags and flowers and cheering and crying, and it was nice to see the Union Jacks and it felt like we were finally getting closer to home-sweet-home.

From Colombo we sailed for Aden. The Arabian Sea was rough and the old *Devonshire* had no stabilisers and wasn't nearly as big as the *Asturias*. There was a lot of rocking and rolling and sicking over the side. But I was alright for some reason. It was like I found my sea-legs down in the stinking hull-cell on the way out. It was night when we arrived in Aden and we had no shore leave, which was probably just as well, after the belly-dancing episode on the way out. Then on through the Suez Canal and a final stop at Port Said before the last leg of the journey to Southampton. It was night-time in Egypt as well, so no shore leave there neither.

But it couldn't be as simple as that, could it? The weather was rough again in the Bay of Biscay and the ship was diverted to Liverpool due to some diplomatic brick-dropping and that put another two days onto the journey, because the Irish Sea was in a terrible rage over us British soldiers trying to sail through it. We finally disembarked and lined up single file for customs and were told to empty our kitbags. This got on my nerves a bit because we'd been out in a war zone and now these bloody customs curmudgeons were searching us for fags and contraband booze. I felt like punching one of them right in his pork chops – but I didn't. I was bringing in cigarettes alright, but I'd given 400 of them to a mate who didn't smoke. So, apart from the hassle of having to unpack everything and repack it again, I got away without paying any duty. And rightly bloody so! We had a meal and a cup of tea and boarded the train for London. When we got down to Hertfordshire, the train passed through Hemel Hempstead but didn't stop, and I wanted to pull the emergency cord and jump out and run across the tracks and kick my heels in the afternoon air. But I resisted the temptation and we carried on to Euston station in London, and this is where we split up and went our separate ways to the various barracks where we joined up. My mate Jock was heading for Northampton and I said goodbye to him and I've never seen him since. I hope he reads this book and remembers me.

I arrived at Bedford station at 1600 hours and boarded a three-tonner bound for Kempston Barracks. As we were being demobbed the next day, we were allowed into town that night. A group of us did just that and headed straight for the Silver Cup pub, which was in the High Street at the time. I was spinning round the moon and back again about being home in the counties – and I wanted to celebrate. We had a whip-round of a pound apiece and, at 10d a pint, this was enough to get us well started. After a while, we went top-shelf at 1s/6d a nip and played darts and sang round the piano and were having a right old time altogether until we heard the landlord shouting.

'Time, gentlemen, please!'

We were well steamed by now and found a café across the street that was still open and we all went in for a right old slap-up. I said I'd pay for it, as I was feeling flush after the booze and

I wouldn't be seeing any of them again after tomorrow, and we had steak and chips and it came to £1/17s/6d for the lot! Fancy remembering that!

Outside, we were waiting half-dibby-like at the bus stop until a bloke came strolling by and gave us a look.

'The last bus is gone, lads.'

So we had to start shanks's-ponying it back to the barracks. We were all wanting a piss by now and some were feeling a bit sick, but there was no public toilets anywhere. So we went into this garden and slashed and sicked up against the hedge. Then a top window opened and this voice came screaming out.

'I've called the law. I'm fed up with you soldiers pissing up my hedge!'

We took no notice, but a mile down the road we were overtaken by a copper on his bicycle. He was laying the law down and reading the riot act and his face was going more purple than it already was from trying to catch up with us on the bike.

'But we've just come back from Korea, Constable.'

He stopped in full flow and looked a bit sheepish.

'Well … alright. But don't let me catch you doing this again.'

'We won't …' then, under our breath, '… let you catch us.'

'Otherwise I'll have to arrest the lot of you.'

With that, he slung his leg over the crossbar and rode off on his law-enforcing way.

By the time we got back to the guardroom, we were twenty minutes late and the jumped-up little corporal of the guard decided to put us on a charge. After an early breakfast, I was told to report to the regimental sergeant major's office and I thought, bloody hell, they're gonna keep me here for another twenty-eight days. But, after a serious bollocking, the charge was dropped and I made my way to the guardroom to sign out for the last time. I got into a 15cwt truck and was taken to the train station, and when I climbed out of that lorry it finally felt like my illustrious career in the army was over. I'd ended up a seven-star private – with one star for everything I did right while I was in the army. Which was some achievement, considering all the things I did wrong. I could've been a corporal or even a sergeant if I'd wanted to. But it wasn't for me – I was too much of a maverick for the chevrons.

I arrived at Boxmoor station at 11:00 a.m. and walked the four miles home with my kitbag over my shoulder and it felt the same as when they finally let me out of the reform schools, all them years previous. I got to our house about noon and went indoors and kissed my mother. She always had the teapot bubbling away on the stove, so I sat down and had a jug of java and a chinwag with her and I was just on my second cup when my spoilsport of a father blustered in.

'Ah, you made it at last, Ken. I'll have a cup too, Kate.'

That's all he said – no 'welcome home' or 'happy to see you, son' or anything like that. He sat down and I knew what was coming next.

'Right, Ken, we're working on Mr Fleming's new garage workshop in Markyate. When you've drank your tea, you can make your way over there and give the boys a hand to finish off the gable end, so I can pitch the roof in the morning.'

It was no use me saying I'd just come back from Korea, because I knew it wouldn't cut wood. I had no civilian clothes and the brothers had worn out all my working duds, so I jumped on my motorbike and made my way to work in my uniform. I got stuck in until 6:00 p.m. and that was my first day back in Civvy Street.

Come the weekend, I went down to Johnny Bates's tallyman shop in the Old High Street in Hemel and bought a suit and shirts and shoes and socks for work and it all came to about thirty quid. Johnny did everything on tick and I gave him £2/10s as a deposit and promised to pay five shillings a week off the balance. My father was building himself another new house, which wasn't far from the old one – only about a hundred yards down the lane. He started it the Saturday before I arrived home and it was already above the first-floor joists. It was Friday when I went to work on it and, by the afternoon of the next day, Dad was pitching the roof with my brother Dave, and by seven o'clock that night it was finished. By the time the tilers came, at 7:30 Sunday morning, Dad and Dave had fixed the staircase and started laying floorboards. The electrician and plumber came next and by mid-afternoon they'd done their first fixings and the cesspit had been dug out the back and the base concreted. On Monday, brother Bill, Bill Green and myself laid 3,000 rough-work bricks lining the cesspit and then shuttered and concreted the top. It took only twenty-one days to build that house from top to bottom and my family was able to move in – although we still had the garage and garden walls to build.

This was typical of my tight-fist father to cut costs to a

minimum and with me and my brothers working for nothing as well. After all, it was our house too – or so he said. For wages, we were expected to work on other jobs at the same time as doing the freebie on our own house. We built houses for my brothers Bill and Dave and Peter and Alec the same way, for free, and I thought I'd get one too when my turn came. But that wasn't to happen because they wanted a mortgage deposit from me and I was wild and will-o'-the-wisp and didn't want to pay up, and by the time I settled down and saw the sense of having my own little castle all to myself, it was too late.

At about the same time, we were also building a house in Cupid Green, on the left side of the road near Three Cherry Trees Lane. This was a big, three-bedroomed house and myself and old Ernie Cox, who was seventy-six at the time, dug out the footings and all the drain runs. I thought I was fairly good on a fork and shovel until I worked with old Ernie. We were digging in clay and he made me sweat every day doing that groundwork by hand and I suppose I'd gone a bit soft from skiving in the army.

'This is hard work, eh, Ern?'

'Put the shovel in the bucket of water, like I showed you.'

'OK.'

'See, the shit just slides off.'

'Still hard work, Ern.'

'Hard work, Ken? You boys don't know hard work these days!'

Ernie had worked on the chalk ground at the Bennetts End site, and the flint and pudding-stone at Northchurch, and he knew the meaning of hard work alright. After concreting the footings and manhole bottoms, I started the brickwork up to dampcourse, knocking up all the muck by hand and carrying bricks ourselves, and even Ernie had to admit *that* was hard work. Then two days later, my brother Bill and Bill Chapman came to give us a hand and brought a mixer with them.

Easy, eh?

15

Naked Through the Ridings

I saved all my army pay in Korea, because I was making enough money with my hair-oil and drinking water and all the other little business bonanzas I ran and, anyway, there was nothing much to spend the wages on. So, I had a nice little lump sum of £300 when I got back home. The army only wanted to give me £130, but I knew I had more than that coming. I queried their calculations and they upped the total to £210. But I queried that figure too and they went away and fiddled the books again and made me a final offer of £300, which I had to accept as it was take it or leave it. But it just goes to show that even after I was demobbed the British Army was still trying to diddle me out of my dues.

Me and John Wells stayed good friends when we demobbed and another mate of mine was a chap called Sid Sells. John Wells and Sid Sells – that rhymes and it's a bit like that old joke, What's the difference between Bing Crosby and Walt Disney? Bing sings and Walt disnae. Ha ha ha! Now, I forgot to tell you this, but when me and John were on leave together that time when we worked for my father and nearly felled the tree on top of his flat-back, John took me round to his house in Ebberns Road and I saw his sister Jean for the first time. She was ironing in the front room and I looked into her eyes and something moved inside me and I don't know to this day if it was love at first sight for Jean – but it was for me. I never said nothing at the time, but I told John how I felt when we got back to barracks and he said I should write to her – which I did. But she wrote back and told me I was too late, she'd met someone else. And that was that, I never got another chance because she was married when I got out of the army – and to a fella who was the exact opposite of me. And I often wondered what would've happened if I'd been brave enough to tell her how I felt the first time I laid my lascivious eyes on her.

Anyway, me and John Wells and Sid Sells were like the three bad boys of Hemel Hempstead at the time. John had a brand-new BSA-250 classic motorbike and Sid had a BSA-350 Goldstar and I bought a black BSA-500 with my demob money from the army – that was us, three geezers on our BSAers! We were the holy terrors of the highways and byways round Hertfordshire. After buying my new motorcycle, I felt like Jack-the-Lad again, like I did back in 1950 after getting my first bike – twenty years old and after seeing half the world and an amazing machine under me, paid for in cash, and finishing off my apprenticeship as a brickie and cocky as a tree full of fruit-chucking chimpanzees.

I took a bet I could get ten blokes on my bike at the same time and, after the pubs closed one night, I did just that. Me driving and three on the back and three more hanging off the sides and two on the handlebars and one on the headlamp, and I rode up Berkhamsted High Street. But I was pulled by the police for having no lights because the bloke sitting out front had knocked it off with his foot. I was taken to court and fined two shillings.

John Wells was courting one of the girls who worked as skivvies at a private school over in Berkhamsted, the next village north from Treacle. These girls came from Middlesbrough and, as it was summer holiday time, they were going up home for four weeks. John had the bright idea that the three of us, him and me and Sid, should bike it up north for a weekend and we said, 'Why not?'

So, early on a Saturday morning, we hit the road for the wild and windswept precincts of North Yorkshire. We rode at a steady 60mph, only stopping for a bit of breakfast and the occasional roadside piss and we arrived in Middlesbrough at 2:30 p.m. John's girlfriend Maggie arranged for us to stay at some relative's house and we stowed our gear there before hitting the high spots. Now, I don't want to offend anyone from the North, but this particular part of Middlesbrough was a total dive of a place and it took us half an hour to even find a decent café. John had already arranged to meet Maggie at 7:00 p.m. so, after gobbling down the grub, me and Sid found a pub and decided to wait there for them. We ordered a couple of pints of mild and Sid paid.

'It's cheap up here, Ken.'

'How much?'

'One and six for two pints.'

I took a slug from the glass.

'Now I know why it's cheap, Sid.'

'Why's that, Ken?'

'It tastes like chucken piss.'

'We'll get used to it. Cheaper than the chicken piss we drink down south.'

By now, a few of the local midnight cowboys were playing darts and I'd never seen a dartboard like the one they were throwing at before. It had no trebles and the doubles were twice as big as the ones we were used to. But I was always up for a challenge and I fancied trying my luck on it.

'Put a K up there, mate,' I said to the big bloke taking chalks. He gave me a rough old look and then turned to his mates with a Geordie accent.

'We got a cockerney bastard in the pub!'

'Leave it out, Mac.'

His mates weren't amused and I just gave Mac a friendly smile and thought, one more remark like that and we'll see who's a cockerney bastard. Anyway, I took chalks and played Mac at 501, double start and finish. Mac threw first and got an eighty away. I took my throw and scored three double-tops. Mac came back at me with another eighty and I threw three more double-twenties. He tried hard to catch me up but I got too far ahead and finished the game with two double-tops and a bull's-eye – I wasn't chief sharpshooter in the army for nothing! Mac didn't like me winning, but he said nothing for now.

Someone suggested we should play doubles and Sid and I partnered up and never lost a single game. This went on for over an hour and the two of us was getting a bit merry on all the free beer we were winning and all the time this Mac was giving me the hard stare and I'd had enough of his sullenness. I said to myself, 'I ain't waiting till I'm dropping down drunk and then getting ambushed by this big stupid smoggy[15].' So I went nose to nose.

'You want to go outside and sort it?'

'No need for that.'

He took a shot at me and I ducked to my left and he hit one of his mates in the mouth. I came back and buried my right in his gut and he bent over and I gave him the left elbow into the snout. Blood was flying everywhere from his bust nose and he went down onto the floor like a sack of spuds and nobody else weighed in to help him. It was just about then that John Wells came back with his girl Maggie. She took one look and said, 'Who put Mac to sleep?'

'This London lad called Ken.'

He didn't say cockerney Ken, so I let it go. Maggie came over and gave me a kiss on the cheek. Apparently this Mac was the local hard man and a big bully and she'd been waiting for someone to lay him low for a long time. The others never articulated no opinion, so I assumed they felt much the same way and there was no more trouble. Mac was taken away to have his schnozzle reset down at the A&E.

The pub closed at 10:00 p.m. and we made our way back to the café and had some late-night fish'n'chips before heading back to where our beds for the night were waiting. I thought John might be sleeping with Maggie, and me and Sid would have the room between us, but they weren't allowing that kind of pre-

15 Teesider.

marital fornication up in uncompromising Middlesbrough – no more than they did anywhere else in those days, so it was the three of us to two single beds and a bundle of blankets on the floor. We decided to toss for the floor and, after several unsteady pitches of the pennies and inebriated arguments about how and where they landed and even losing some down between the floorboards, Sid ended up with the short straw and me and John had the bunks. After about half an hour in the bed, I woke up scratching like a mangy dog. I put the light on and had a look and saw that the sheet was covered in fleas. They were big brown buggers and so many of them they were marching in formation and ready to launch another attack on my arse. I woke the other two and showed them the state of what I was sleeping on.

'That's it, I'm off out of here!'

'Where to, Ken?'

'Home! You coming?'

'Not likely, it's too late.'

'See you later, so.'

With that, I grabbed up the rest of my gear and walked out in my vest and underpants. I stowed my clothes in the pannier bag on the side of my motorbike and hit the road south at 2:30 a.m., riding in my shoes and socks and windblown bloomers. After about fifteen miles or so, I stopped beside a stream and stripped off completely and lay in the water to get rid of any alien fleas that were planning on coming south with me. I took all my clothes out of the pannier bag and washed them too. Then I tied them to the pillion seat and sat down and had a cigarette. When I was finished, I put my crash helmet on and rode the bike stark bollock naked for the next fifty miles, through towns and villages, until my clobber was dry enough to put back on. I stopped again at the side of some road, had another cigarette in the nude, and then got dressed. And I wondered what might an innocent passer-by have thought if they'd come across me there, standing at the side of the road in the naked paleskin, with fag in hand and dongles dangling – or maybe they were used to that sort of thing in the rural ridings. I got on the bike and rode as fast as I could, back to civilisation, and swore never to set foot back up north again – until they fumigated the place.

By the time I got back from Middlesbrough, after riding all through the night, it was opening time and I went in for a few pints to the Wagon and Horses pub in Hemel because I was in bad need of a libation. Then I went home and had a wash and a change and rode on over to Berkhamsted to see if John Wells was back yet and to tell him he could stick the north of England up his arse from now on. John wasn't anywhere around, so I wandered into the Goat pub and met this man in uniform called Sear, which was the same name as me, only without the S and no relation. I bought him a pint and we got talking about the army and I told him I was in Korea and one drink turned into two and so forth and so on. Now, the Goat had a separate section for teenagers who were too young to drink alcohol, but they could bring their own records to play and have a dance. They called it the 'long room' and me and Sear could hear the foot-tapping music so we wandered in there. The place was bopping and blowing blue notes and we were just stand-ing back and watching the jiggers and the jivers.

Then I saw her – this girl – she had jet-black hair and she was the most beautiful woman I'd ever seen and I fell instantly in love. Even more instantly than I fell for Jean Wells. I turned to the soldier.

'Do you see that girl?'

'I do.'

'She's beautiful.'

'You want me to introduce you?'

'You know her?'

'She's my sister.'

And that's how I met Marie Sear — with the same name as me, but without the S on the end and no relation whatsoever. Who would've believed it? It was the summer of 1954 and it wasn't all that great weather-wise — dull and damp and not all that much sun. But, for me, it was the most wonderful summer I ever experienced. Nothing like it came before and nothing like it would come after either. I asked Marie to come out with me on my brand-new motorbike and she accepted my invitation and I think she might have been a bit star-struck because Marilyn Monroe thought I looked like Kirk Douglas and I'd been away fighting in Korea and places she'd never even heard of and was the coolest and hippest of all the eligible boys in the whole county. And I took full advantage of her admiration.

We went out regularly after that and she took me to see her mum and dad. The old man was called Albert and he was seventy-one years old when I started courting his daughter. He'd served in World War One and was one of the men who suffered from mustard-gas poisoning. When the Great War ended, he went to work for the local gasworks and then for the British Gas Board and

My lovely Marie when I met her as a teenager.

you'd think he'd have had enough of gas from the trenches and not gone anywhere near it again, but he never missed a working day in the whole of his life. We got on from the start because we met in the Crooked Billet pub in Gossoms End and he liked a pint and a game of darts and so did I. Marie's mum, Irene, was a lot younger than him because he was married before and had three previous children. Marie had one brother, who introduced us, and three sisters, one even younger than her who was called Yvonne. Old Albert might have been muddled up by the mustard gas, but it didn't hamper him much in the area of his hydraulics.

Anyway, me and Marie were inseparable all through that summer and it was about August time and we were out roaming round on my motorbike of a Sunday afternoon when we came across this field full of haystacks. I was feeling randy as a buck-rabbit and we parked up the bike and went into the field and got down to business underneath one of the stacks. Now, normally, I would've had a packet of Frenchies, but this day I wasn't prepared for the sudden urge that came over me and neither of us understood much about the menstrual cycle or the reproductive period or the fertilisation free-for-all, so we decided to take a chance. After it was over, we sat back and had a cigarette and accidentally set fire to the straw and had to shift ourselves out of there sharpish as the whole haystack went up in a huge blaze. We watched from a hill overlooking the field as the fire brigade came out bell-ringing and hose-spraying and the farmer hollering and hand-waving in case the flames spread to his other haystacks and maybe even to his farmhouse as well.

About five weeks later, Marie went to the doctor and found out she was pregnant. She was crying when she told me and I held her and said not to worry and then she admitted she was only fifteen – and the legal age of consent was still sixteen. Even back in 1954. You could have felled me with a wet fag-paper – she looked so much older when I first met her that night in the long room, with her black hair and beautiful face and film-star figure. I should have known, because all the girls of age had proper drinks and the others were sipping soda water, but you don't think of these things when you fall in love at first sight. For the second time. And she didn't tell me because she was afraid I wouldn't go out with her and if she had, maybe I mightn't have – no, that's not true.

There was never any question but that I'd marry her and I went down the Crooked Billet to tell old Albert after a fair dose of Dutch courage first. But he was alright about it, as long as there was going to be wedding bells, and Marie's mother Irene wasn't too upset either. But I could tell she might have been a bit disappointed and wanted her daughter to wait a bit longer before having a babby to bring up. But she said nothing about it and it was settled that we'd tie the knot in January – after Marie reached sixteen on Christmas Eve and I got to the two twenty-ones – 21 January and my 21st birthday.

Next to be told was my own family, but I only wanted to break the news to my mother and leave telling my father until later. Mum made me a cup of tea and I sat in the old man's rocking chair, trying to be all serious and stoical-like. But the chair tipped backwards and I threw the tea all over myself and it was dripping off my chin. Mum got me a towel and she was half-expecting something like this to happen and it was only a matter of which girl I put up the spout first. But she was reasonably happy when I told her how much I loved Marie and that there'd never be no one else for me. She promised not to say anything to FW until I was ready to do it myself.

But Marie's doctor reported the pregnancy to the police and the coppers paid me a visit because she was under the age of legal consent. I told them I was going to marry the girl and her people were happy about the arrangement and, after looking me up and down and scowling at me a few times, they left it at that. The old man was characteristically sarcastic.

'Did you have to put her in the family way?'

'Yes. Just like you did to Mum.'

That shut him up and he never mentioned it again afterwards. I kept on courting Marie and John Wells was still seeing northern Maggie and we travelled back and forth to Berkhamsted together on our bikes. It was well into autumn now and the year was rolling on and I was soon to become a married man and, after that, a father for the first time. And my wild days would be over and I'd have to well and truly settle down and stop jacking-the-lad all over the land and half the world as well.

On Christmas Eve 1954, me and John Wells were over in Berkhamsted seeing the girls as usual. It was Marie's sixteenth birthday and our love affair was now legal and we'd been for a drink and a dance at the local village hall to celebrate. And in those days you weren't allowed to stay over at your girlfriend's house, even if she was four months pregnant. So, when we dropped the ladies off, we went back to John's house in Ebberns Road for a late one. We were just putting the glasses to our mouths when we heard this scream coming from the back of the house. John said it was cats fighting, but I wasn't so sure – so I opened the back door. We heard the scream again, coming from across the canal. It was a female scream. We ran across the hump-backed bridge and saw a woman on the ground with this bloke on top of her and it looked like he was trying to rape her. I ran as fast as my boozy feet would move and hit him a flying fist in the face as I skidded past. This knocked him off the woman and he landed out cold with a lustful look in the one eye that was still open and staring skywards. John ran to the nearest phone box and called the police, while I went to see what state the woman was in. She was a bit hysterical and I didn't recognise her until later, in the light of the police station, and I was keeping an eye on the would-be rapist as well, in case he came to and tried to leg it.

The police arrived quickly and arrested the bloke and they took John and myself to the station in Bury Road to give a statement. A doctor was there examining the victim and it was then I recognised her as old Mrs Weston – a local eccentric woman who dressed up in costumes she made herself to celebrate the pagan festivals of Beltane and Hallowe'en and the equinox and solstice. She'd ride round the village on her bike in the regalia she made and the bike would be decorated as well – maybe as a maypole with streamers, or the sun or the moon or even with her as St George and the bike done up as a dragon. She was at least sixty if she was a day and I couldn't for the life of me understand why the geezer would want to rape a woman of that age. But, then, I was only coming up to twenty-one and sixty was out of the Ark as far as I was concerned.

A woman of sixty would be wishful thinking to me now – ha ha ha!

After making our statements, we were told we'd have to appear at the local courthouse on Monday to give evidence. The failed rapist was an Irish bloke who was fresh off the mailboat and Mrs Weston had already said in her statement, 'he was just going to enter me' and the magistrate insisted that I should repeat those exact words.

'I can't say that, you honour.'

'I am not your honour, I am your worship . . . and why not?'

'I'm embarrassed.'

'We have heard everything in this court, Mr Sears. Now, was he just going to enter her or not?'

'He was.'

'Say it!'

'He was . . . just going to . . . enter her.'

'Thank you, Mr Sears.'

Then he adjourned the case because the Irish bloke had pleaded 'not guilty' and was remanded in prison until the next hearing in Berkhamsted Court in three weeks' time. In the meantime, old Mrs Weston kept chasing me and John round the town on her bicycle to measure us up for a pair of jumpers she wanted to knit for us as a thank you for helping her in her 'hour of need', as she put it herself. We wouldn't go anywhere near her, but she eventually caught up with us and we had to wear the pair of matching plain-grey, cable-knit pullovers. She said she wouldn't give us money because, in her own words:

'You boys would only use it for the devil's purposes.'

At the next court hearing, the rapist testified that he'd been to midnight mass and couldn't remember what happened after he left the church, as he was paralytic drunk at the time.

And what was Mrs Weston doing out at that time of night?

On an early-hour Christmas morning.

Without her bicycle.

But then I had to say, 'He was just going to enter her,' again and he pleaded 'not guilty' again and the case was adjourned again. I had to repeat the obnoxious phrase one more time before the case was eventually adjourned to the opening session of the Cambridge Assizes Court in March 1955, which is the same as the Crown Court now. Me and John were taken over there by the police and we experienced the opening ceremony of the quarter session in all its flippery and finery. Three High Court judges and barristers and clerks and all sorts of judicious jokers in their wigs and gowns and led by the Lord Mayor. The town crier banged on the door of the courthouse and someone opened it for him and the session was in sitting for the following three months. I wondered what would've happened if nobody was inside to open the door – would they all have said 'sod it' and went off home? Anyway, we were sitting there all day because the judges had to be sworn in and that took hours and we were pacing up and down the witness waiting room and I wasn't looking forward to having to say them words again – in a bigger court this time and it might even be quoted in the newspapers. But the usher came out after a long, long while and told us the rapist had changed his plea and we wouldn't be needed to give our evidence after all.

We were directed to the account clerk's office to get paid our expenses and the little turd-faced twat asked me how much I wanted to claim.

'Three half-days' and one full day's money at bricklayer's rate of 6s/6d an hour . . . plus petrol.'

He looked at me like I was an escaped lunatic.

'We can only pay a maximum of £1/10s a day.'

I tried to reason with this pen-pushing prick but his answer was 'take it or leave it'. In the middle of our argument, a doctor walked into the office and the clerk fawned all over him and said 'certainly' when the quack gave him a bill for forty-two guineas. I was apoplectic about this, so I said to the doc, 'Do you think it's fair we only get thirty bob a day and you can claim forty-two guineas?'

'No, it's not fair. I should get more!'

I swore out a string of bleeps and the clerk told me if there was any more language like that, I'd be held in contempt of court.

The failed rapist got twelve months, which I thought was a little lenient, considering all the trouble he'd caused, and John and I left. I made a vow never to offer help to the legal establishment again. Even when I later knew about another Irishman who was shagging his landlady's chuckens. He was eventually caught hen-handed when the landlady noticed the chuckens weren't laying eggs and hid herself to see what was happening. The Irishman got sent to prison and it was in all the national papers.

Fancy having to give evidence at *that* trial!

16

Fatherhood is Rather Good

M arie and me got married on 22 January 1955, the day after my 21st birthday, at 10:45 a.m. at Berkhamsted Register Office. I didn't celebrate my 21st because I couldn't afford that and a wedding as well. The registrar had to look twice at the name – Kenneth Sears marrying Marie Sear, without the S at the end. He could hardly believe it and we had a job to convince him this wasn't a covert attempt to legalise incest. Not all that many people attended, just Marie's immediate family and my brother Dave and John Wells and Sid Sells – that was it. There was no photographer and no presents and no confetti and no cake. Afterwards, Marie and her mother and sisters walked on home and the men went down to the Goat pub for a drink. Don't get me wrong, it was the same for most working-class couples back then, nobody had much of anything because the last of the rationing after the war had just ended six months previous. So we didn't feel sorry for ourselves if that's what you're thinking.

We went to live with Marie's parents at first, but that didn't last long – just about eight weeks. Don't know if it was my fault, but I just couldn't get on with her mother. Then we went to live with my parents, but that was just as bad and lasted about a similar length of time, because I just couldn't put up with my father making cynical comments. Our lovely daughter Deborah was born on Friday 13 May 1955, and she came bouncing into the world a bundle of curls and crying. But this happy event coincided with my twenty-eight days compulsory Territorial Army training coming due and I had to ride all the way down to Salisbury Plain in Wiltshire on my motorbike and I didn't want to be there – not one little bit. After the signing in, I told my mate Bob 'Blueboy' Hoar that my wife had just had our first babby and I wanted to be with them both, not here playing at soldiering. I told him I was going to leg it back home on the bike and asked him if he'd cover for me and call out my name on muster in the morning. Bob was alright with that, so I buggered off as soon as their backs were turned. I went straight to see Marie at St Paul's Maternity Hospital in Hemel Hempstead, thinking she'd be happy to see me. But she didn't appreciate the fact that I'd skived off from my compulsory training and she gave me a right telling-off altogether. Did I mention that Marie was as straight as a screwdriver and didn't hold with no shenanigans or nothing at all like that? She didn't drink nor tell lies nor gamble nor pull strokes like me – and her only lapse of concentration was letting me get near her under the haystack in the summer of 1954. So, she gave me a good old bollocking for slipping away into the wistfulness and shirking my duties to the TA.

But despite her chiding, I still stayed from Thursday to Sunday because, don't forget, in those days women were kept in hospital for a week after giving birth, although I wasn't there for the actual birth, it not being the done thing back then. I got back to Salisbury Plain in time for reveille early on Monday morning and I stood beside Blue in the parade line.

'Everything alright?'

'Yeah.'

As a way of paying back Blue, I had my Uncle Doug make up a couple of clipboards for us while I was secretly AWOL, so we could doss around all day, looking like we were doing something. If you had a clipboard in your hand and looked all official, people were reluctant to ask what you were up to, in case they got roped into something they didn't relish. So, unless we were on specific duties, we walked around all day with these clipboards and nobody came next or near us.

We did have a mock battle while I was down there in Wiltshire. It happened to be on Derby Day and Sergeant 'Peddler' Palmer held a sweepstake on the race and I drew a horse called Phil Drake, a French thoroughbred ridden by Freddy Palmer. I wasn't happy with this, first of all because it was a French horse and I had an aversion to things Français after the dark and deadly glasshouse in Seoul, and second because the jockey had the same name as our drill sergeant.

'Hey, Sarg, you want to swap horses? Mine's got your cousin riding it.'

'OK, smartarse, I'll have it.'

When the race was ready to start, we got the radio operator

to tune in to it and, would you believe it, Phil Drake won. I could've spat six-inch nails! Peddler laughed and laughed and called to everyone:

'Hey, will ya look at Sears' face! Ta, Sears, I'll have a good piss-up on you tonight.'

'Hope it chokes you . . . sir!'

I met loads of mates from my army days down on the TA training and made other friends as well – from Watford and north London and all over that area. This was the teddy-boy time and there was one lad in with us called Johnny Woods. He was from Chipperfield and he'd spent a year growing his hair into a quiff with a duck's-arse stuck out the back and he refused to have it cut. He was the only TA teddy-boy to ever be court-martialled and he got sentenced to six weeks in Aldershot glasshouse. The *Daily Mirror* got hold of the story at the time and it appeared on the front page – it also ran in all the Sunday papers. Johnny did his time and came out with his quiff and his DA intact and he became a local hero in the towns and villages around Hertfordshire and never had to buy a drink in any pub in Chipperfield ever again.

I wonder if he's still around – and if he's got any hair left.

When I got home from the TA after the twenty-eight days, it was straight back to work with my father. Marie and me and Deborah moved into a caravan on the Happy Days caravan site in Wigginton, close to Tring in Hertfordshire. The caravan was located in the middle of a wood, with overhanging trees and stuff dropping on the roof in the middle of the night. It was cold and spooky and it frightened Marie half to death, so every morning before going to work I had to take her and the babby to her mother's because she wouldn't stay there alone – and bring her back every evening when I finished. It was me on the motorbike, with Marie in the sidecar holding the babby, and the pram strapped in between. One morning a farmer was moving his cows and we ended up in the middle of the herd and all the beasts banging against the sidecar and Marie and the babby screaming their heads off. So I knew we'd have to move somewhere else.

Like I said, the malaria kept coming back to me every year after Korea. Dad didn't believe I could have a mosquito-borne disease in Treacle Bumstead and thought the old woman was laying on my shirt tails. But our family doctor was ex-army and he recognised the symptoms and, when FW rang him, he confirmed I had malaria and should stay indoors until it passed, which didn't impress the old man all that much – but then, nothing did. His construction firm was getting bigger and, as well as private houses, we were taking on work for Hertfordshire County Council, building police accommodation. We were also building cottages for the Crown Estates all over the county and even in Bedfordshire as well. My father bought eleven acres of land in Tile Kiln Lane with a deposit of £400 and made the rest of the £4,000 price by building and selling two private houses in Wood Lane End. Things were looking good and we had enough work to stretch us out for at least the next ten years to come. We were building one complete house per week, a record rate for anyone back then – and it wouldn't be heard of now. At this time, we were still the only major building contractors in the area, because the boom-time of the 1960s hadn't started yet and Hemel

Hempstead was only growing at a moderate rate – nothing like what was to come when the Irish firms moved in on our turf and the town expanded into the small city it is today.

1955 was a good year for building: no frost and mainly fine and buyers were found fast for the first thirteen houses on the Tile Kiln Lane site. We also got the contract to build Wood Lane Garage, in Maylands Avenue, and my father decided to buy himself and my oldest brother Bill a couple of new cars. The old man still had his ancient Morris Cowley but it was out of commission, so him and Bill bought two Vauxhall Crestas at a cost of £1,000 each. By the summer of 1955, the thirteen houses fronting Tile Kiln Lane were built and occupied and FW had plans for the building of sixty-eight more, both detached and semi-detached, on the rest of the land. But this meant the construction of estate roads. My father's plan was to build another detached house and two semis and then start on the roads and services.

The council had other ideas.

The houses were at the brickwork stage and joinery and other materials were being delivered and all trades making good progress, when the council served a notice that all work must stop immediately until the roadworks had been carried out. The old man ignored this notice and kept us working and the detached house was at roof-plate level and the semis at joist level when the council got nasty and took court action. While I was in the army, F.W. Sears & Sons changed its name to F.W. Sears & Son – singular – and the firm became a partnership between my father and my brother Bill. So the two of them had to go to court and all the work at Tile Kiln Lane had to stop. They pleaded guilty in court but the old man defended his actions and they only got a fine of £8 plus court costs, which was pretty lenient in anyone's opinion – but I think it was because the local court had never had a case like this brought by the council before and they didn't know what the penalty should be, so they took a tolerant stance on the issue. I stayed away, in case I was called to give evidence and had to say something about somebody being about to enter someone.

But it put the mockers on any more work being done on the Tile Kiln Lane site for at least the rest of that year, because the old man didn't have the money to build the roads after buying his new cars and he couldn't sell the houses until they were finished and he couldn't finish them until he built the roads. There was also a lot of baahooey blowing about over the Suez Canal and finance was tight and there was a squeeze on credit. As you'll know, President Nasser believed the canal belonged to Egypt and Anthony Eden believed it belonged to Britain and a huge amount of military equipment and troops were transported across to sand-land and I was glad I wasn't still in the army and out there with the long-shirt-lifters. It was all sorted out with Eden giving in to Nasser and Britain losing the canal in the end, but it affected the work here at home and made things difficult for us bare-fisted builders.

Anyway, my father decided to sell the Tile Kiln Lane land, and all responsibilities for the roads and other regulations, to a bigger firm of Wembley builders called Lancaster & Son Ltd – on condition that we would still build the houses and they'd pay him £1,800 for each. He estimated that he could make a profit of £200 per house and, with sixty-eight houses, he'd come out of it with about £14,000 and Lancaster & Son Ltd could have all the headaches of coping with the council. But before he could sign on the dotted line, he got an alternative offer of finance and postponed accepting the Lancaster & Son deal. Unfortunately, and well against the grain, the old man got hustled into signing a contract for the finance without first reading it. He trusted the people involved and they screwed him – the Lancaster deal was better, but after signing the contract he couldn't back out of it.

Me and my little family moved out of Happy Days at the end of the year and into one of the cottages in Chapel Street, Hemel Hempstead, owned by my father. He charged me nine bob a week rent, the old skinflint – a far cry from his promise of my new house being built next, as a reward for all the free labour I gave him on building his and my brothers' places. And so, 1956 came round and we were still working our wigs off, despite the Tile Kiln Lane tits-up. The financier sent people in to build the roads and we started back building the houses. The weather in the spring of that year was ideal for construction and all the houses were up by the summer. But the profit my father made out of it, after all the hard work, was only a quarter of what he would have made if he'd stuck with Lancaster & Son. It must've wrinkled his wallet, because he didn't like to be wrong – and especially to be proven wrong! FW then did another deal for land in Redbourn, close to Hemel Hempstead, a plot with enough room to build thirty-two houses. We rolled up our sleeves and erected the lot in eighteen months but, again, the terms of the deal weren't all that favourable to FW and he made very little profit – or so he said.

During that year, Marie was pregnant again and our second special daughter, Janet, was born on 22 December 1956. Marie went into St Paul's Hospital again and I was at work, just like I was when Deborah was born. We had sex that morning because people were advised by the Health Service in them days to keep having sex right up to the birth and that suited me. I went home at lunchtime to see how she was getting on and she wasn't there. The bit-of-the-other must've had an effect on Marie, because her waters broke soon after I went to work and she had to run down the hill from Chapel Street to St Paul's and she just got to the hospital in time.

The winter of 1956/57 was kind to us builders and 1957 was another busy year, with loads of contracts and lots of hard work. My sister Ann had been working as a clerk for the firm, but she decided to get married and my father needed someone else to run his office at Two Waters Road. He advertised the job and took on a Mr Harrison, who said he had twenty years' experience as a builder's clerk, and FW agreed to pay the man £13/13s for a five-day week. Dad wasn't exactly ecstatic with Harrison's work, but the bloke was competent enough and the old man decided to give him a fair shot at it. Now, in 1957, I decided I'd had enough of working for my father's firm and decided I'd like to have a go of it on my own. I'd tried to do this several times previous, but my father always managed to talk me out of it so he could keep his cheap labour. But this time I was determined I wanted my cards. FW had a look round the office, but he couldn't find any insurance cards, so he said he'd get Mr Harrison to sort them out for me in the morning.

Next morning, the old man got to the office at 10:00 a.m., after visiting the various sites, as was his habit. But the doors were still locked. When he went inside, he found a note from Mr Harrison, saying he knew he'd been rumbled and he was away on his toes to London. There was a big envelope on the desk with all the insurance cards in it, but none of them were stamped. Harrison had only been drawing the insurance stamp money every week at the same time as the wages, but he was padding his pocket instead of stamping the cards. The missing stamps came to a total of £700 and the old man went purple-faced and called the police. The coppers said it was a case for CID, who came round the office and took the unstamped cards away with them. But this wasn't the whole of it. When he checked the books, my father found that Harrison had also duplicated holiday pay, with one lot for the men and one lot for his shady-self. Petty-cash payments were drawn twice and the whole fiddle grew to over a grand – a lot of money in those days. The police told my father that Harrison had been sacked from other jobs on account of being a bit corrupt and that he should have checked the man's references. This was the second mistake FW had made in such a short space of time. He wouldn't admit it, but I knew he could've kicked himself.

OK, I know a lot of this stuff isn't directly my story, but I just want to show that my father could sometimes be naive in his dealings with dodgy people, even though he considered himself to be a clever man with money. If it hadn't been for me wanting to jack the job and go on my own, Harrison might have fiddled a lot more out of old Frank William Sears – clever as he thought he was.

Harrison was arrested and hauled in front of the magistrates. He pleaded guilty and asked for the extenuating circumstances of his large family to be taken into account and a few other hard-necked excuses as well. He was jailed for three months.

I didn't leave my father's firm in 1957, despite wanting to because I'd had enough of my brother Jim. He was a brickie like me and we worked together for the most part, but he was a miserable sod – a single man and all he had to keep was his cock, but he never stopped moaning and I'd had enough of him and wanted to leave. But Dad put me on a different job, so I stayed. Later that year, the partnership of F.W. Sears & Son was reformed into a limited liability company, with three directors – FW, my eldest brother William Albert and my other brother David John, who was next son in the line of succession. I was way down the list of grace-and-favour and would never occupy the throne – I knew that and it's why I wanted out. The year went on with the company buying another plot of land, close to the Tile Kiln Lane development, on which eighty-four houses could be built altogether. But only a third of the land could be drained into the existing sewer for immediate building – the rest would have to wait until proper services came that way in the inflating near-future. Still, despite the setbacks suffered by my father, work was plentiful and things were going good for me and my little family.

Houses on the Tile Kiln Lane development.
The semis sold for £2,400 each.

In 1958, the business moved into plush new premises in Hammer Lane, Hemel Hempstead. The place had a good compound and loads of room for equipment and a carpenter's shop and other buildings as well. Business was booming and Dad could afford to splash out the £8,500 it cost for the lease, plus fixtures and fittings. We later built a four-bedroom, ultra-modern flat over the offices at Hammer Lane and my brother Dave and his family moved in there after selling their house in Wood Lane End. By now we had the best of modern equipment and our own tipper lorry and a drop-sided truck and a maintenance truck and a few 15cwt vans and my father made a promise to himself never to ask for outside finance again, but to build everything with the company's own money, then all the profit he made would be his. My father was, at last, a happy man – king of a construction empire that had been built with the sweat of his sons. And, while some of his sons benefited from this going-up-in-the-world – others didn't!

My third delightful daughter, Heather, was born on 29 April 1958. This time Marie didn't go into hospital and Heather was born at home. This was an option available under the Health Service and I was there for the birth and it was the most wonderful thing I have ever experienced. It's something every man should see at least once in his lifetime – what a woman has to go through to give birth. I know it's what happens normally nowadays, but back then it was rare for a working man to be under the feet of the midwife and I only agreed to it because I already had two children and couldn't afford the time off from work while Marie was in the week-long hospital. But I was glad I did. The emotion was something sublime, seeing new life coming into the world for the first time since the gooseberry-bush delivery in Korea. It was as close as I could ever come to a religious revelation – apart from that time in the Black Forest with the nuns.

The company bought thirty-eight acres of land at Newton Longville, near Bletchley, but we were only able to get planning permission for five detached houses, which were built quick and bought even quicker. The rest of the land was flat and had all services and was ideal for building – it could have accommodated at least 300 more houses and the whole plot only cost the old man

£5,500, which he paid for with company funds and didn't have to involve crooked financiers or banks or any other cajoling crooks. But, despite our differences, me and my brother Jim were working more efficiently than the three 'directors' ever did and knocking our nuts off for the company and getting no recognition for it. But we did it because family is family and we believed we'd be rewarded some sweet day for our loyalty and labour and the pound a week FW stopped from our wages when things were very tight.

Another good construction year came with 1959 – weather was good for the most part and we were building a school in the Tile Kiln Lane area. Houses were easy to sell in those days, because London was overspilling and Hemel Hempstead was only half an hour away by car and there were good rail and road links to the capital and also to airports like Luton and Heathrow. Old Treacle Bumstead was rapidly becoming an ideal commuter location and the 1960s were looming. With all this potential and expansion, other building firms were attracted to the area and competition was beginning to grow – especially from the Irish. With the boom in building came an increasing scarcity of land. When the village was small, there were plenty of fields around – but now the available plots were beginning to disappear, what with industrial workers moving out and small factories being built. And, as with everything, when something is scarce, its price goes up.

My father's and brother Dave's houses in Wood Lane End became the subject of a compulsory purchase order, at the cheapest prices possible, by the Development Corporation that was supervising the building of the New Town of Hemel Hempstead, and Dad bought a nice plot of land in Leverstock Green to put up a new four-bedroom house for himself. The Development Corporation planned to build an industrial estate on the land it requisitioned, but this never materialised, and when Dad and Dave moved out, the council rented out the houses to executives and made a big profit. The houses were top quality and are still there to this very day.

Work on Dad's new house started just before Christmas, and almost immediately the weather closed in. Freezing frost replaced the rain and brought all work to a complete standstill. This applied to all the jobs, not just the family house, and it lasted well into 1960. Heavy snow followed the frost into the new decade and my father had to lay off a lot of his men. The bad weather held its grip on us until early March, when the heavy rain and floods that followed the snow started to abate at last. But it was really April before the worst of the weather finally cleared off and left us alone to get on with our building. Father's house was finished in the summer and he sold up in Wood Lane End and moved in in July. Dave also sold up and moved into the flat over the offices in Hammer Lane. Despite the shortage of land, my father always seemed to be able to find some for sale and his building empire was expanding all the time.

He bought a big house called 'Tall Trees' from the film and television actor James Hayter, who played Friar Tuck in the 1952 film *Robin Hood and His Merrie Men* and later went on to act in *The Forsyte Saga*, *The Onedin Line* and *Are You Being Served?* The house was huge and had enough land around it to build twelve others. The old man paid £21,000 for the whole kit and caboodle and he reckoned he could sell the existing house for £6,000 as well as making money on the new-builds. But when James Hayter moved out, the vandals moved in and smashed the windows and doors and ceilings and ripped up the floorboards. As well as that, the Aga cooker in the kitchen was damaged when the local yobs and yokels tried to make off with it, and they half-inched a lot of the fixtures and fittings while they were at it. The damage was so bad that the whole house had to be pulled down and a new one built in its place. This cut drastically into the old man's estimated profit on the 'Tall Trees' deal.

We started work on 'Tall Trees' before Christmas and things were going well until the New Year. Then the job got jinxed. A monsoon of rain fell in January and February of 1961 and conditions on site were miserable, to say the least. The site had a subsoil base of heavy sticky clay and the rain turned it into a quagmire, slowing up everything. A colossal amount of reduced digging was necessary, meaning any hills had to be levelled off, and the surplus earth had to be moved from the site. It was impossible to get lorries in because they got bogged down in the soft clay and it was also difficult to use a mechanical digger, and you'd walk out of your wellingtons, stuck in the clay and mud. But the drainage excavations had to go on, despite the weather, and the excavated earth had to be pushed up into heaps, to be taken away when the conditions improved. This meant double handling and more heartache for my father. We couldn't sell the surplus on as topsoil because it was all just shit clay after twelve inches down, so we dumped it into dell-holes and cavities left from the old brick kilns. Weather conditions did improve towards the end of February, but the water still lay in large pools on top of the clay subsoil, causing even more headaches. But we carried on and seven houses were well under way by June 1961.

Then the bloody summer turned wet as well and this slowed things down on all the company sites, and it didn't let up until the autumn. In November, our general foreman, Bob Nicholas, came into the office and it was obvious he wasn't all that well. His face was deathly pale and my father told him to go home and get straight to bed. Dad wouldn't let him drive the van and got one

The Sears Boys, at our Gran's 80th birthday, 1961. Back row: Peter, Jim, Bill, Dad, Alec. Front row: Dick, Dave, me.

of the other men to go with him – that's how bad he looked. His condition got worse on the way home and his wife called the doctor. About an hour later, my father got a telephone call to say Bob had died of thrombosis – he was only forty-three. As if in mourning, the rain started again and all work on the 'Tall Trees' site had to stop and couldn't be started again until the end of January 1962.

17

Cement-Mixer Serenade

My father-in-law, old Albert Sear — without an S at the end — got stomach cancer and finally died in 1962, after being bedridden for eighteen months. Sometimes, if I was round the house, I'd help turn him over to make him more comfortable and couldn't help noticing how bad his bedsores were. But he never complained about nothing — right up until the last couple of weeks of his life. By then, the doctor was coming in three times a day to give him his morphine and I heard him whisper once when I was close to the door:

'Can't you give me enough to put me out of my agony?'

But the doctor just shook his Hippocratic head and left him to linger. The following Sunday evening, I took Marie and the girls over to see her parents. Marie's sister Yvonne was there and her brother-in-law Peter came round to do some work in old Albert's garden. Well, Albert only got himself out of the bed after eighteen months of being on his back and he walked into the room and spoke to Marie's mother.

'Just going down the garden, Irene, to see if everything's alright.'

We all thought it was a ghost at first and, before we could close our open mouths, he was on his way down the path to see Peter.

'It all looks lovely, Peter.'

That's all he said. Then he turned round and left poor Peter as shocked as the whole set of us. He walked into the house again and never said nothing to nobody, just went back to bed and closed his eyes and died.

Then, on 27 September 1962, my first and only son, Trevor, was born. I was as chuffed as a cat in a creamery. I'd already agreed with Marie to keep having kids until I sired a son and now he was here and I had more than a few pints to celebrate his arrival into the world. The contraception pill came out as soon as Trevor was born, so we could have sex on a Sunday afternoon without having any more babbies and that's what we decided between the two of us to do. Trevor turned out to be a good boy and, over the years, I taught him everything I knew about the building game. He was also very mechanically minded and could take a whole motorcar apart and rebuild it when he was just a young lad. Today he's a man I'm very proud of and he can turn his hand to anything and I love him a lot – as I do all my children!

In November of 1962, my father had a change of heart and he called me to his office in Hammer Lane.

'You still want to go self-employed?'

'I do.'

'Alright, I'll teach you how to do it properly.'

He said he'd show me how to keep my books balanced and take out tax and insurance and holiday pay and all the other adding up and administration. I said I could get a clerk to do all that kind of codology.

'Remember Mr Harrison?'

'Yes.'

'That's why you need to know about these things for yourself!'

It wasn't out of the goodness of his heart – he knew by going self-employed I'd have to work harder and he'd get his jobs done quicker, but he taught me how to cost and estimate and measure up for amounts of brick and blockwork and know what plans and blueprints were all about. He taught me everything I needed to know to go out on my own in the building business and so began a new leaf in my working life. But, although I was officially self-employed from November, I stayed working on my father's jobs as a pseudo-subcontractor until the start of the tax year in April 1963.

That's when I went legit and became 'Ken Sears – Brickwork'.

But, as soon as I struck out on my own, the terrible white winter of 1962/63 descended upon me and my master plan. I got up at 5:30 a.m. on the morning of 27 December and cleaned out the front room fire grate to get it lit for Marie and the kids when they climbed out of bed. I took the ash and clinker to the back door to sling the stuff out and when I opened it I was confronted

with a solid wall of snow, well above the door head. At the time
I was still renting the two-up-two-down cottage in Chapel Street
from my father and it had an outdoor khazi and coal shed. The
problem was, how to move all this snow and clear a pathway for
my little family to go and have a pee and then to get fuel in to
light the fire. The obvious solution would've been to walk out the
front and make my way round the back. But when I opened that
door, I was met with another solid wall of snow. I scratched my
head and made a pot of tea and took a cup up to Marie.

'You might as well stay in bed, love, till I work out how to get
out of the house.'

I opened the bedroom window and looked down. The snow
had drifted on our side of the street and it was up to the win-
dowsill and spread over the front garden and only dropped down
in drift height at the edge of the road. And the only thing I had
to move all this snow was a little black short-handled coal shovel.

I went again to the back door and started shovelling – a little
snow at a time, putting it in the sink and letting the water run it
down the plughole. I also dragged over our tin bungalow bath
and filled that up to the top. It took me until 10:00 a.m. to get to
the toilet and open the door. Luckily, the night before I'd lit a hur-
ricane lamp and left it in the loo to stop arses from freezing to the
loo-seat and this was still working. Then I cleared the snow from
the coal bunker and brought in fuel and built a fire to warm the
house and our frozen hearts. By now the kids were up and wanting to go out and sling snowballs with the other chavvies in the
street. They thought it was all a big adventure, of course, but it
was a bloody nuisance to me. After breakfast, I dug my way

through more waist-deep snow with the little coal shovel to get to the garage, where my van was parked. It took me another two hours to manage this, but once I got inside I was able to get hold of a proper digging shovel and clear a route to the road. Then I had to jack the van up and let some air out of the back wheels, so I could wrap five thick rope-ties round each one and then pump them up again to tighten the traction. With all this done and a little more shovelling, I was able to get out of the back yard and away from the snow-white street.

I went up to Dad's yard in Adeyfield and he told me there was no work and I'd have to sign on the dole like the rest of his sub-contractors.

'I got four kids, Dad . . . I can't live on the dole!'

'Alright. Look, I'm going to offer two lorries and some men to the council to clear snow. You can drive one of them.'

'Thanks.'

'I should give it to someone else, as you don't work for me no more.'

But he didn't. The council paid us a small amount of money for clearing the snow and, topped up with the toad-in-the-hole, I was just about able to make ends meet for my little four-kid family. We worked from 8:00 a.m. till 12:00 noon and cleared the town centre first, then parts of the new town, like Warner's End and Leverstock Green and Gadebridge. But that work only lasted a couple of weeks and there was still nothing moving on the building sites, so I had to start relying solely on the rock-and-roll – and my wits. And that's when the old wayward ways of my boyhood came in handy – skills like ferreting rabbits and poaching pheasants and half-inching food from farmers' fields. I also went round collecting returnable bottles, and soda siphons were even better because you got 2s/6d for them. I'd even nick empties from the backs of unprotected pubs and run round the front and resell 'em to the bar staff. It was a tough time and you had to do whatever had to be done.

I was out of work for twelve weeks altogether, and even when I did get started again the ground was so frozen the labourers couldn't dig out the footings, even with the help of a JCB. The thaw took another week or so, before I could get back to the jobs I was working on around Newton Longville and Stewkley in Buckinghamshire. I had two men hired up called Ron Fry and Nobby Bisney and the work took us six weeks to finish. After that, we started to build a house at Orchard Close for my father's firm. But after two weeks, Dad called me into the office and told me, because of the bad weather, no bricks were made during the winter and now there was a severe shortage.

'I can't get no more till September, Ken.'

'It's only May . . . that's no good to me, Dad.'

'Listen, Ken, you have enough bricks to build two houses. That should keep you going.'

'Keep *me* going, alright, but what about Nobby and Ron?'

'You'll have to let them go.'

This was like a kick in the teeth for me. I'd only just started up on my own and I was having to lay men off already.

It was a tough decision for me and I didn't want to do it, but I had to think of Marie and the children first. All my father said was, 'Now you know what it's like to be the boss.'

I slept on it overnight and in the morning I managed to make contact with another subcontract bricklayer friend who had a bit of bodge and he took Ron and Nobby on – it was only supposed to be temporary, but they stayed with that firm for many years and never came back to me. I often wondered why. But it worked out well in the end and I carried on at Orchard Close on my own, building the two houses. I started work at 6:00 a.m., loading out bricks for an hour and putting up the corners. I'd go home for breakfast at 8:00 a.m. and then back to work knocking up muck and laying bricks and standing up door and window frames and setting up the scaffolding. I'd go home for dinner at 6:00 p.m. and go back after dinner and work till 9:00 p.m. I carried all lintels up to seven foot long on my shoulders and used a bogie to bring the heavy nine-foot lintels in under the scaffold, and then I raised them up on two sets of blocks until I got them through the bottom of the tower. I used the bogie again to wheel them into position and then jacked them up on the blocks until I could place them on the brickwork. This was hard going and it took a full twelve hours to do.

While I was working away like this, my father came on site to see how I was getting along.

'Jesus, Ken, why didn't you ask me for some help?'

'You told me to let my men go.'

'I don't want you having an accident.'

'I won't have an accident.'

'Look, Ken, I used to have to work like this when I was your age, but there's no need for it nowadays.'

'Put my money up, then.'

'I can't do that!'

So I carried on as I was going and completed the pair of semi-detached houses by the end of August, a time of ten weeks.

F. W. Sears & Son company van. I was no longer part of
the company but I still worked with Dad.

By then, more bricks were starting to trickle through and I was able to put the word about in the local pubs that I was looking for brickies and labourers. I got my little gang up to four brickies and two hoddies and I was asked by a man called Harry Valentine if I was interested in taking on twenty houses at a big site in Stanmore, in the north London borough of Harrow. Harry worked for McManus, who were a big firm of Irish builders, and if I was to subcontract for them I was expected to supply my own mixers and spot boards and hosepipes and hoists. I could include all these extras in my price but, at the time, I didn't have enough dough to go out and buy them to start the job – unless I could get them buckshee. But a twenty-house contract was too good for a small starter-upper like me to turn down. So I had a word with a mate called Dave Wandsworth.

'You got forty quid, Ken?' he asked me.

'Sure.'

'And you got a pick-up truck.'

'Sure.'

'Well, there's this building site in Stanmore—'

'I'm starting on a building site in Stanmore,' I told him.

'There's two building sites in Stanmore . . .'

As it happened, my brother-in-law John, married to Marie's step-sister Gwen, had a pub in Harrow called the Corner House and me and Dave and a mate of his went for a few drinks there the following Friday night. I told John what we were up to and we'd need access to his pub later in the night for an alibi. So he called the police and told them he was having a private party after the pub shut, just in case they came snooping. We drank until 11:30 p.m. and then left to do our shopping. The building site was about two miles away and when I got there I discovered that it also belonged to McManus, the people I was going to subcontract to on the Monday.

'Dave, they'll know it's their gear.'

'Not if we paint it a different colour.'

And it was too late now to go anywhere else.

The place wasn't locked up and there was no security. The petrol-driven hoist was three floors up, so we first dismantled it and lowered it down onto the back of the pick-up and hitched the wheeled section up to the hindquarters. The pick-up had no tow-bar, so we had to tie the thing to the bumper and it was sliding from one side of the road to the other, all the two miles over to the other site where I needed it for first thing Monday morning. We then went back to 'borrow' the mixer and water barrel and hosepipe. We tied the mixer to the back of the pick-up and towed it, but it had no tyres on the wheels, just iron rims. It made a racket like a clog-dance on a corrugated roof and we had to pass the police station in Stanmore, which was located right in between the two sites. We went as slow as we could passing the cop-shop, without making ourselves too conspicuous, but the bare wheels on the mixer still rattled like a wrought-iron tractor and we might as well have been rag-and-bone men ringing a peal of bells. Still, not one copper even looked out the window to see who was dragging a dozen tin baths through their town and we thought they must all be asleep.

After depositing the rest of the gear at the site where I was to start, we went back to the Corner House pub and my sister-in-law let us in by the back door.

'Police.'

'Where?'

'In the public bar.'

Once the coppers heard there was going to be 'afters', they decided to come across for a drink themselves. No wonder they never heard us passing with the iron-wheeled mixer! But if they saw us coming in now and McManus reported the missing gear, they'd smell a rat. Gwen had the answer.

'Go in the toilet and come out one at a time. I'll put your drinks on the bar in the lounge and it'll look like you've been here all night.'

We were able to do like she said because the place was as big as a barn and it had five bars and you could easily get lost in it. We stayed till four in the morning and sang to get ourselves seen and even played darts with the police. What an alibi!

Next morning, Dave came round and gave me a hand to paint the grey hoist and mixer blue and fit a couple of old bicycle tyres onto the iron wheels – for camouflage. I paid him his forty quid and a twenty for his mate and it was money well spent. On the Monday morning, I took four bricklayers and two hod-carriers and four lads from the local labour exchange who were posing as labourers to the site and we erected the blue hoist – just to show the guv'nors we had a good gang together and we'd be well able to take all the work up to joist high on day rate, and they said the rest of it would be on a price. I met the men from McManus's office on site at 10:00 a.m. and it was agreed I could take on the work at £10 per man until it was up to the agreed level, and then negotiate a price for the rest of the job. I also got an agreement that the hoist and mixer would be paid for by them at a rental rate of £7 per day. They never even noticed that it was their own equipment.

After the head-office men left, the site agent called me into his hut and I knew well what the snake-in-the-grass wanted.

'I like to earn a few pounds out of the subbies on this site.'

'I don't know what you mean?'

'Don't play the gobshite with me.'

'Alright.'

'How many dead men you want me to book in for you?'

'Four.'

'OK, and I'll take two.'

I gave the four lads from the labour exchange a fiver apiece and told them they could go home. But I wanted them to turn up every Monday morning and I'd give them another fiver for each time. I paid the men on site £8 a day, making £2 from each of them, plus the money for the hoist and mixer and the four dead men. A nice little deal. Then I left my foreman bricklayer to run the job while I went off to work for my father.

My father worked on the same principle as McManus, that all subbies supplied their own gear, but in my case and on account of me being his son, he supplied the scaffold. Although I had to include erecting it in the price I gave him. I got together another gang of four brickies and two hoddies and gave them a price per yard, including scaffolding. After making all the money I could from McManus on the day rate, I buggered off before the price work started and sold the hoist and mixer for £150.

Things were going well and I was making good money – so I decided to buy a new Morris Oxford motorcar at a cost of £715 for cash.

Life was sweet.

Marie and me had our first holiday that year. We took the kids to Yarmouth by the sea from the Friday night of one week till the following Friday morning of the next. We toured all over Norfolk and had trips on the Broads and visited the village of Wroxham, not far from the Red House Farm School where I'd been as a boy. I wanted to see the reform school again for some reason, so we went there and stood outside and I was going to go in. But Marie didn't like the idea and thought it might be bad luck, so I turned round and walked away. I wish I hadn't now.

We also visited the seaside town of Wells-next-the-Sea and the kids loved this place because they could paddle out for nearly half a mile and the water only came up to their waists and the sea was a clear green and not cloudy like Yarmouth or Cromer. We fell in love with Sheringham and the little bakers who made all the bread and cakes while you waited and you could see them flinging the flour in front of your eyes. We always went back to Norfolk for our holidays after that – and most of my family still do. But the time just flew past and Friday morning of the next week came too quick and we had to pack up and leave at seven o'clock that morning. We arrived back in Hemel Hempstead at 11:00 a.m. and I drove round my two sites and paid my men and went straight back to work.

One thing about when I was on site – the kids would always come to 'work' with me on the weekends and I'd give them little jobs like stacking bricks on the ground floor oversites, and they loved doing this until they got bored. Then I'd let them roam round the fields with our dog, Tom Tucker, and this would carry on all through the summer holidays from school. The girls were about seven and nine and ten back then and I know it wouldn't happen now with all the abductions that's going on – but I loved to roam round myself when I was young and before I went into the reform schools and I wanted them to have this freedom too — at least for a short while in their innocent lives. Trevor was only three at the time and he had to wait a while before getting out with the grass between his toes and the sky blue up above and the wind blowing the life into his little lungs.

Darts outing to Clacton, 1962. I'm standing fourth from left.

18

Fitted Up by the Turn-Ups

My dog, Tom Tucker, was a black-and-white bouncing-up-and-down mongrel with a big curly tail. He stayed on site with me most of the time, no matter where I was working. He could climb up ladders, but not back down again, and could balance on ledges and roofs and guttering like a mountain goat and he could catch fish and do all sorts of tricks that most other dogs wouldn't dare to do. I must have sold him at least half a dozen times to people who'd see him on site climbing up the ladders and they'd take photos of him and ask if he was a circus dog and if I wanted to sell him. I'd get a fiver a time for him and tell them to keep him indoors for a few days until he got used to his new home. But I knew he'd whine and whimper to get back on site and they'd let him out after an hour or so of howling and he'd jump the fence and run back to me. I'd hide him for a few days until the hullabaloo died down and then sell him again to the next lot to like him.

My father formed a new company, which was separate from
F.W. Sears & Son Ltd. He called it 'Factory & Property Maintenance' and I worked for that company as a subbie on the building
of the big industrial estate in Hemel Hempstead. We were hired
to bed in new machinery during the two weeks summer holiday
closedown of an engineering plant called Dexion. The pits for the
machines had to be dug down four foot and then backfilled with
three foot of hardcore and one foot of concrete on top to take the
weight of the machines and the pounding and pummelling of
them when they were operating. Well, after the digging out and
bedding in of the machines, I left the labourers to the backfilling
over the weekend and had a few hours off to spend hugging my
family. While I wasn't there, the half-eejits only went and used
the old rubbish from the pits instead of the hardcore and the
machines sank when they started banging and bumping and had
to be dug out and reset. And I got the blame, all because I took
a few hours off over the weekend. But that was the way with my
father, he'd blame me before he'd blame anyone else because it
was easier.

A lot of people remember the 1960s as swinging and sexy
and full of employment – and it might've been like that in the
first half of the decade, but the second half was a bit more
bloody. At least it was for me. From the time I left my father's
firm and went self-employed in 1962, up to 1966 when England
won the World Cup, my little firm of 'Ken Sears – Brickwork'
was doing well and dancing and, at the height of my fame, I
was employing upwards of forty men at any one time. But this
all changed for two reasons. The first was big construction firms

At the Crazy Horse pub on a beano in Margate, 1964.
I'm the worried-looking cowpoke on the far right.

like McManus moved, like boomtown rats, onto my patch in Treacle Bumstead and they undercut the smaller outfits and forced us further out of the area. I had to look for work in London and Beds and Bucks and had to cut my prices to the marrow to get that work. The pubs in Treacle were full of tough, Irish builders and so-called 'hardmen' up from London who did bouncing on the doors of the clubs that were opening in the new towns like Hemel and Stevenage and Welwyn Garden City, and some of them carried shivs. I had a few run-ins with one or two, but I was fit and fearsome and could handle myself with the best of the bullies and anyone who wanted to wade into me usually came off second best. So it got to be known – 'don't mess with Ken Sears'.

And, after a while, most of them didn't.

Selective Employment Tax was the other reason that sent me spiralling out of business. It was introduced by Harold Wilson's government in the mid-1960s and had the effect of killing 'Ken Sears – Brickwork' off overnight. You might not believe this, but back in those days, most building site workers were on PAYE, not self-employed like they are today. SET ordered every legitimate subbie to buy a 'holiday' stamp for each man he employed, costing £4/16s a week. On the other hand, Irish workers were allowed to graft for eleven months of the year tax-free, as long as they went back to Macushla for the other month – and this was called 'the lump'. I couldn't increase my prices to cover the cost of the SET stamp – I had up to forty men working for me on half-a-dozen sites at any one time so you can see how much of my hard-earned it was costing me. Neither could I compete with the Irish, who were pulling all kinds of cash-in-hand strokes on the lump and getting away with green murder. The only alternative was for my men to go self-employed, but none of them wanted to do that, believe it or not, because it made them feel insecure. Nowadays you'd have to use a ball-squeezer to get any building worker onto PAYE. So, I had to shut down all the sites and go back working on jobs for my father with a small two-and-one gang.

From 1967 onwards, work in the building trade got slower and slower and I was earning less than I was in earlier years. I took on work in north London doing the brickwork on a big site of five-storey blocks of flats. These buildings were shuttered up and concreted on the inside, with four-and-a-half-inch brickwork built on the outside. The shuttering carpenters nailed tie-irons to the inside of the boarding and hung the ties to face into the concrete. When the shutters were struck, we dug the ties from the front of the concrete and built them into the brickwork – this tied the concrete and brickwork together. However, when I reached the top of the third floor, I noticed the carpenters hadn't fixed any ties in the concrete for the last two floors. So I shot down to the site agent's office.

'The wood butchers ain't put no ties in for the top two floors!'

'Who's running this bloody site, Sears?'

'You are.'

'So get back on the scaffold and lay bricks!'

I could see he was in no mood to manoeuvre, so I did what he said and kept laying bricks until I got to the top of frame head level. I could see all the brickwork moving at the slightest gust of wind and I knew what would happen if it really started to blow, with only the roofing sections and the windows holding the whole thing together.

As soon as I got weighed in that week, I took the cheque to the bank and paid ten bob to have it expressed. Then I went back on site and paid my men and jacked it in. I said if any one of them wanted to take the rest of the work on, I'd sort it with the site agent on Monday. I lost the week-in-hand that was owed to me and I was out of a job. Later on, in the 1980s, there was an enquiry into the amount of heat being lost from these flats on account of cavity walls without insulation. The London Borough of Brent decided to fill the cavities by pumping vermiculite into them. This was done by drilling holes in the bed joints of the brickwork and blowing the tiny particles of phyllosilicate in under pressure. Which worked well until they came to the top two storeys where no tie-irons had been used and the outside brickwork started bulging under the extra pressure, so they had to stop. The only way to put the problem right was to re-scaffold and take down all the brickwork and frames and have special ties made and the concrete drilled and the ties plugged and screwed into it. Then the brickwork had to be rebuilt and this process must've cost the borough council a fortune – and all because an obstreperous site agent wouldn't listen to me all them years previous when I tried to tell the simpleton how to run his site.

But this was the very middle of the 1960s, and I was getting on a bit by now – thirty-two and with a wife and four children to feed and having to work hard for every shilling I earned. So I didn't feel much like swinging. But the post-war days were over and the young people wanted to live and forget about the 1950s and who could blame them. Popular music was all the rage and a new thing called a teenager came into the world – stroppy and shouting and with a few quid in its pocket and able to influence trends and television programmes, and the world was its watering-hole. The Pill had been around since 1962 so sex was easy to have and not get knocked up, and hanging was abolished in 1965 so you could get away with murder as well as mayhem. All sorts of recreational drugs came out, like speed and amphetamines and marijuana and LSD and you didn't need a bellyful of beer to get happy no more. But it all came a bit too late for me; I'd already sown my wild oats and now was the time of bringing up my children to sow theirs.

Then the Land Levy was introduced by the Labour Government in 1967 and land prices immediately went up, making it more costly for builders to buy plots for development. The idea was, if a landowner gained planning permission to convert agricultural or commercial land for residential use, he'd be in for a big windfall of millions of pounds and the Land Levy was seen as a way for the government to get their hands on some of that dosh. So, the greedy guzzlers put a tax on plots of land that were bought to build on. It was another stealth tax and all that happened was the landowners held back selling their land to builders and the shortage of land drove the prices up further and caused a slump in the building trade. As well as that, the tax turned out to be very complicated and expensive to implement, so they had to scrap it because it cost more to administer than it brought in in revenue. But it didn't make things any better for me at that time and I had to scratch about all over the place to make a crust of bread.

1968 came and, as usual with a new year, we all hoped it would be better than the last. And it was to begin with. I kept myself and a labourer busy building garden walls and small extensions and other short-term stuff, but nothing big enough to make a man rich. So, I went and did a stupid thing. It was around June time and I was having a drink with a mate of mine who for the purposes of this story I'll call Joey Price in the Royal Oak pub at the end of Hemel Old Town and he asked me if I was interested in nicking a safe.

'Whose safe?'

'Alf Norton's, he used to run the Queen's Head.'

'I know Alf, where's he now?'

'Retired and living in a bungalow in Pitstone.'

'Nah . . . I don't think so, Joey.'

'C'mon, Ken, it'll be a doddle.'

The safe was supposed to have £5,000 and a sackful of gold sovereigns in it and, as the evening wore on and I had a few more pints, the prospect grew more appealing and I never thought of asking Joey how he knew there was five grand in cash and a gross of gold sovs in the safe.

By now it was just gone 8:00 p.m. and we drove over to a pub in Pitstone where old Alf and his wife were known to have a drink. Sure enough, there they were in the saloon bar and I sat down beside them for a chat and a chinwag, while Joey went over to their bungalow to spy out the lie of the land. As it happened, the back window was open, so he got in and managed to get the safe out into the front garden. But it was too heavy to lift into the car, so he came back for me to go give him a hand. Now, any normal-thinking individual would be worried about leaving a safe standing on the front lawn of a house, but not Joey – and not me neither after all the ale I'd had. We made an excuse and disappeared for half an hour and loaded the safe onto the back seat of the car. Then we went back to the pub and had another drink with Alf – just so he wouldn't suspect anything!

After an appropriate length of time socialising, we said we had to take our leave and the landlord asked me if I'd do him a small favour.

'What's that, Des?'

'Take Paddy home when you go. He's drunk as a skunk and he's a bloody nuisance when he gets like that.'

I forgot about the safe on the back seat.

'No problem.'

Joey kept nudging me and kicking me in the shin, but it was too late to renege by the time I realised what he was trying to tell me. Then he decided to have another drink and wait for me, because he didn't want anything to do with this Paddy bloke – or so he said. It seemed to me Joey didn't want to be in the same car as a hijacked safe and a drunken Irishman, so I had to take him home on my own, with the safe on the back seat beside him. Luckily enough, he was so stocious he didn't even notice it. But it was a job getting him out of the motor and I had to help him across the road to where his wife was waiting arms-folded at the garden gate. She straightaway belted Paddy across the face and near knocked him out. Then she took a swing at me for getting him drunk, which I didn't, but I ducked and she missed. I legged it out of there as fast as I could in case someone called the cops, while she dragged the semi-conscious Paddy down the path. When I got back to the pub, the door was locked and I had to knock to get in, which wasn't exactly inconspicuous. Joey was still there drinking with Alf, so I had another pint and then said we'd better be going.

Joey drove the car down to John Freeman's garage in Flaunden and we used his cutting gear to open the safe. There was only £500 in cash and 36 sovereigns and 25 half-sovereigns, along with 10 gold dollars and 10 half-dollars. There was also some cameo jewellery that wasn't worth much and we put it in a tin box and buried it on Ivinghoe Beacon. There was also about 150 silver thruppenny bits that I threw into a plastic petrol can in the boot of my car. We fenced the sovs and Yankee dollars and a few other gold trinkets to a bent jeweller in Paddington for £450 and the whole thing made us less than a grand – a far cry from the £5,000 plus there was supposed to be in the stupid safe.

We were arrested at half-twelve in the afternoon on the following day, just after getting back from flogging the gold. It was a Saturday and we were taken to Hemel Hempstead police station and charged with breaking and entering and burglary. Alf Norton told the police in his statement that there was £3,000 in the safe, along with six full sovereigns and six half-sovereigns. He never mentioned that he'd bought himself a new Rover car the day before with the rest of the money that was supposed to be in his strongbox and it was obvious to me he was a crook himself and trying to claim back cash he'd already spent. It was also illegal to hold more than half-a-dozen gold sovereigns at the time and he conveniently forgot how to count up to eighty-one, which was the total number of gold coins in the safe and took him well over the legal limit he was allowed to stash. The reason we were arrested in the first place was because the coppers asked Alf who he was drinking with that night and me and Joey were the only two who weren't locals in the pub and that was enough to throw suspicion onto us. They interviewed the landlord and he backed up old Alf's story – even after I helped him out and took the drunken Paddy home for him.

He deserved a clout for that, if I could've got close to him!

We were held on remand at St Loyes Street Prison in Bedford and our case was listed to come to court in September. And this was only June. But before I go on, I have to tell you about my younger brother Alec, who was only twenty-six at the time. A few years earlier, Alec was driving along the A41 when he collided with a lorry. He fractured his femur and was in hospital for a while and had to have several operations. The end result was, his left leg was an inch or so shorter than the right one and he had to wear a built-up boot. Anyway, in July 1968, while I was on remand, Alec was working on one of my father's sites where there was a shortage of bricks. There were two bricklaying gangs on the job, Alec's and the Cox brothers'. Before knocking off for the night, the labourers from each gang loaded up the scaffolds with their share of the bricks for the next day. But the Cox brothers' man came back later and nicked most of the bricks from Alec's scaffold station. Next day, of course, Alec didn't have enough bricks, so he had to go and work inside. The house wasn't under cover, so the floor was slip-slidey and they were walking on scaffold boards over the joists. Alec had to wear wellingtons that weren't built up like his boots, so it meant he was walking with a limp. He was carrying a seven-foot lintel with another man when he slipped and the lintel fell and smashed his head. He was killed instantly.

I always blamed my father for allowing this to happen. He should've stood off the other gang and let Alec get on with it. But, just like he used to blame me, it was easier to give in to the ones who weren't family.

My brother Alec on my bike in 1956.

I was allowed out of prison on bail under judge-in-chambers orders and I only later found out that FW put up a £2,000 surety. I had to take Alec's place on the job and I hated doing this because it felt like I was walking over his dead body. Alec's fatal accident affected the family in a terrible way – and no one more so than my father. He died of stomach cancer eight weeks to the day after Alec. Nobody knew he had the cancer and we were told the shock of Alec getting killed like that might have brought it on – he was sixty.

I stayed out of prison until the case came up at Aylesbury Crown Court on 22 September. Both Joey and I pleaded not guilty, but the police produced a suit they said belonged to me –

it belonged to me alright, but it wasn't the one I was wearing on the night of the robbery. They said they found globules of gunmetal in the turn-ups of the trousers that could only have come from the safe that was cut with the acetylene torch. They failed to explain how such globules of molten metal, falling from the melting safe, didn't burn the fabric of the trousers – and the defence barristers didn't ask them. What a stitch-up!

Alright, I know I did it – but I was still stitched up!

So, we were found guilty and sentenced to two years in prison. We were sent straight to Oxford Prison to start serving our time. Oxford was a cramped little hole, the smallest prison in England, that was only used to hold convicts who were to be transported somewhere else. There were three to a cell and we were banged up for twenty-three hours a day, with half-an-hour exercise in the morning and half-an-hour in the evening. Now, I always found it hard to hold myself together in an enclosed space and this place nearly drove me insane – it was like being buried alive. After a month I was climbing up the walls, and if I could've got out they never would've got me back in again. But then I was sent to Gloucester nick, where I had to sew mailbags. It was eight stitches to the inch – seven or nine was no good and would be rejected. I just couldn't get it right and all the ones I sewed were condemned and I never earned a single penny and my fingers were as sore as a sock full of splinters. But at least there was a bit more space and you weren't breathing someone else's arse-air all the time.

I was transferred from Gloucester to Verne Prison, on Portland Island, just offshore from Weymouth in Dorset –

maybe because of the mailbags, I don't know. Verne was originally constructed by prisoners in the 1840s. It was mostly all underground and built of Portland stone, quarried by the prisoners. These stones were four foot long by two foot high by two foot thick. The buildings themselves were about 200 foot long and 50 foot wide and it must have been back-breaking work to cut the stones at the quarry face and then lay them. Just as well I wasn't around in those days or they'd have had me doing it for sure.

Verne was a Category C prison for adult males. The inmates consisted of lifers and certain-length-of-sentence prisoners, mostly serving four years or more – even though I was only in for two. We slept in eighteen-man dormitories and there was no such thing as privacy, even when you went for a dump. But I was used to that from the army and it was better than being banged up in a stifling cell all the time. You couldn't escape because it was an island and there was nowhere to run to – not like in the reform schools, when I could leg it over the wall and across the open countryside. Anyway, I was a lot older now, and you'll say none the wiser, but I knew they'd come after me and catch me and I'd be looking at an even longer stretch. So I got my mind right and told myself to take the medicine and get out as quick as I could. I had a wife and children waiting for me and I didn't want to hurt them any more than I had already.

The prison had all sorts of trade courses the cons could sign up to, including bricklaying and plastering and carpentry and electrics and plumbing and welding and painting. I signed up to do a six-month course in plastering because I thought it'd give me

another string to my bow in the building game when I got out —
and I might as well be doing something as sitting there sucking
my thumbs. I already had some experience of plastering from the
time I was an apprentice, so I had a head start over the other five
men on the course. Our civilian instructor was called Mr
Cheater — I kid you not — and he was a local man from Weymouth. He was a first-rate tradesman and I got on well with him.
As I was way ahead of the others, he suggested I should do up a
door opening and then build an arch into it, which could be used
as part of the training course. He got permission from the governor and I made up my own arch turning-piece and plastered it.
If you're ever in Verne Prison and see the arched door on the
plastering course, you'll know it was made by me.

After finishing the plastering course, I was called to the governor's office and told I had to go before a judge at Leighton
Buzzard Court under a new legal rule called a 'restitution order',
by which any money made from crime could be claimed back by
the person it was stolen from. He said they were sending me up
to stay in Bedford Prison until this was done, and I didn't really
want to go back up to St Loyes Street. But I didn't have a choice.
Two days later, I dressed back in my civvy clothes and was put
in a taxi with two screws. The journey should've taken about
four hours, but it took seven. We stopped at every motorway
café on the way and the screws stuffed their faces with the driver
and they gave me nothing but a cup of tea. Everyone in this café
was clocking me because I was trying to drink the tea with the
handcuffs on and not making a good job of it because the chain
was rattling and everyone was rubbernecking and making me

nervous. Then a customer came over and spoke to one of the screws.

'Why can't you take off his handcuffs?'

'More than my job's worth, mate.'

I piped up.

'D'you think I'm daft enough to do a runner and get caught before I get halfway across the car park and then have another eighteen months added to my sentence?'

So they took the handcuffs off and let me drink my tea in peace.

A few minutes later, the same customer came back with a half-ounce of tobacco, a packet of papers and a box of matches.

'Can he have these?'

'I don't think so!'

The man looked hard at the screw.

'What if I call the Home Office and tell them you un-hand-cuffed a prisoner, against regulations?'

The screw soon had a change of heart. The man gave me the tobacco along with a wink.

'Best of luck, mate.'

And I knew human nature was still alive and kicking – in some parts of the world at least.

We arrived at Bedford nick just after seven that evening and I was checked in. By the time I was issued with prison gear, it was half-past eight.

'Right, Sears, let's get you bedded down.'

'Hang on, I ain't had nothing to eat since breakfast in Verne this morning.'

'The two who brought you in got paid to buy you dinner and tea.'

'If they did, they're drinking that money in the pub now.'

He put me in a three-man cell on my own and, to tell the truth, he went and rustled up some bacon and eggs and beans with a couple of slices of bread and a mug of cocoa. So, it was my day for meeting good Samaritans. Later in the night, they threw two coloured boys from Birmingham into the cell with me. They'd been done for dealing drugs and sentenced to seven years. Next morning, I was moved into a dormitory with younger prisoners and put on a work detail unloading lorries. After that, I was made to reinforce the ceilings of the cells with wire mesh and then plaster it over. This was under supervision of a civvy contractor and he asked me if I'd like to do a bit of overtime. I said I would because I'd rather be doing that than stewing in the stir. After tea, I reported back and worked until 8:30 p.m. The civvy contractor would take his break in the screws' mess room and I'd wait outside. A con came out with a bucketful of dog-ends from the mess ashtrays and I did a deal with him for the butts. I then split the dog-ends and saved the reusable tobacco from them and this came to about an ounce-and-a-half of dross. I was able to swap this for half-an-ounce of proper Old Holborn and I did it twice a week the whole time I was back at Bedford.

While I was there, a local vicar in Hemel Hempstead took Marie and the kids up to see me out of the goodness of his God-fearing heart. It was a nice surprise to begin with, but it ended up upsetting Marie and making the kids cry and then that got me wound up and it went all wrong. So, before she left, we agreed it would be best if she didn't come and visit me again. And the next time I saw her was in 1970.

I was taken to Leighton Buzzard Courthouse after a month and was held down in the same cell the Great Train Robbers were in when they were arrested – I knew this because their names were scrawled on the walls. They brought me up and I paid back what money I had on me when I was arrested – which came to about £500 after flogging the gold. Old Alf Norton didn't make waves, in case the authorities did him for having more coins in the safe than he was legally allowed, and he got another £500 back from Joey Price, so he made money on the deal in the wind-up. About a fortnight later, we finished the plastering in the cells and I was taken back down to the Verne. Before I left, the governor agreed that if I gave my word not to try to escape, the screws would keep the handcuffs in their pockets. I told him he had a deal and we went back by train and I could relax and look at the fields flying past the speeding window.

Back on Portland Island, Mr Cheater showed me how to do stick and rag moulding on a bench and how to run skirting round a room and picture and chair rails as well, and I also learned to make up stick and rag coving for ceilings – so it wasn't all a complete waste of time, because I was a little more cooked coming out than I was going in. And a lot more plucked. During my time in Verne, it was decided to build a new prison inside the old one, using the prisoners for labour, especially the ones who'd learned trades. I was told I'd have to do bricklaying but I didn't want to – I wanted to do plastering so I could practise my new proficiency.

They wouldn't let me, so I asked to be transferred to another prison, one that would make use of my new plastering skills. Within three days, I was transferred to an airfield in Sussex called Northeye Prison. It was like a concentration camp with a wire fence round it, but they put me to work bricklaying again and I complained again. Within two days, I was transferred to Ford Prison in West Sussex and this time I stayed put till the end of my sentence.

19

The Jubilee and Other Jubilations

When I got to Ford Open Prison, I had to work in the garden and on the farm at first and this was really like being back at Red House Farm School – only I was a lot older now, if not any the wiser. Then I was put on a labour gang going down to Portsmouth Naval Prison that was being converted to house prisoners coming to the end of life sentences. They let me do the plastering, so I was happy enough. We got on a bus at seven in the morning and came back to Ford at seven in the evening – like in the film *Cool Hand Luke* only without the chains and Boss Godfrey. Although I'm sure some of the screws would've liked to have had a loaded rifle slung over their shoulders. There was brickies and plumbers and electricians and labourers and plasterers and it was just like being on a building site, only you couldn't go home after work and we were like a free-labour gang.

Like I said, Ford was an open prison and once we got back in the evening, we were free to do what we wanted until nine at night. We slept in ten-man huts and not in cells. I joined the football team and the cricket team because at the weekends they sometimes let us play clubs from outside the prison and the players gave us tobacco and the odd bottle of beer – as long as they weren't seen by the screws. If they were, they got into trouble as well as us and we weren't allowed to play them no more. Prison visitors would hide drink and drugs around the perimeter fence and tell the cons where the stuff was hidden, but I never bothered with this because I just wanted to get back out as quick as I could and not do anything as stupid as robbing the safe in the first place.

With three months of my sentence to go, I was given a day's leave to arrange work for when I got out. But I knew I'd get a start with my father's firm, even though he was dead and it was now being run by my brothers Bill and Dave. So I went home to see Marie and we hugged and kissed and stayed in bed for a long time until the kids came home from school and then I hugged and kissed them and said I'd be back soon – and I wouldn't go away from them ever again. The road back to the prison was sad and solemn for me, and if I'd been single I'd have legged it away across the uplands and downlands and they'd have had to come running after me. But I knew I didn't have long more to go and I couldn't do anything that would hurt my wife or kids again.

It was 1970 when I got out and I don't know how my lovely Marie stayed by me while I was in prison and I made my mind up never ever to let her down no more. I went to work for Bill and Dave like I knew I would, as a self-employed subcontractor.

They put me on a job at Northchurch Common, digging out footings by hand for a garage. The ground was a dog-bitch to dig with a fork and shovel because of the big flints and pudding stones and, after four days of blood, sweat and blisters, I'd only earned twelve pounds. I was also having to board two buses to get to the job and walk a mile from the bus-stop and back again, because my car was impounded at Aylesbury police station and I couldn't afford to go over there and get it out. Sometimes I wouldn't be getting home until nine o'clock at night and so tired I could only eat my dinner and fall straight into a stupor. In the end, I had to ask Bill to put a mechanical digger on the job and I was surprised when he said yes – I think it was more to speed things up than to help me out of my misery. But I was able to get a lift with the digger driver every morning and back home again in the evenings and, once I got a couple of weeks' wages under my belt, I put my Morris Oxford back on the road and life got a bit lighter.

But after two years in prison, Marie and me were stuck in a mire of debt and the work wasn't enough to pay all those obligations off. Now, I was known about town for being a man who could swing a fist or two and I was approached in a pub by a bloke who worked part-time as a bouncer. He said there was good money to be made for a man who could handle himself, so I went doing the doors for a bouncing firm run by a giant called Joey Seabrook. I didn't work much in Hemel Hempstead in case I had to come up against any of my mates and I stuck to clubs in other towns like Welwyn and Watford and Hatfield and other places in Hertfordshire. I also couldn't afford to get into trouble with the law, as they gave me a little time off my safe-cracking sentence for good behaviour and if I did anything naughty, I'd be back inside to finish the time sooner than you could say 'sling him down the stairs'. I did four nights a week for £10 a night, starting at 7:00 p.m. and not finishing till at least 2:00 a.m. – then having to work a hard shift's bricklaying the next day. After six weeks of this, I was dead on my feet and decided to give it up. But at least it went a long way to clearing our debts and Marie took on running a canteen for Kodak & Company at night. She worked from 6:00 p.m. till 10:00 p.m. and made all her own food at home and sold it for a profit as well as being paid by the firm.

While I was in prison, my dog Tom Tucker was shot by kids with an air rifle in Randall Park, which was right beside where we lived in Chapel Street. The pellets lodged in his brain and, when he made his way home, he was in a lot of pain and he turned nasty and bit Marie and she had to have a tetanus injection. She took the dog to the vet, but the pellets couldn't be removed, so the poor old bugger had to be put down. I was so sorry when I got out and found my dog was dead and my wife was bitten and I was inside when it all happened and couldn't do anything to prevent it.

While Marie wasn't a drinker, she used to like going out with a couple of lovely ladies called Mary Joyce and Mary Burke during the 1970s. Marie was a short woman and the two Marys were tall and they used to link each of her arms on either side and her feet would be off the ground as the three of them sauntered down the street. The girls used to go dancing in the local community halls and the Rose and Crown and, although Marie wasn't a big boozer like I said, the two Marys were. I used to collect her afterwards and often ended up round Mary Burke's house drinking with her and her husband and others and partying until the early hours of the morning.

My mother died in 1973 – she was sixty-eight. She was diabetic, but they didn't know and were treating her for something else and it went all wrong. So she died. It was a sad day for me, after all the years of growing up with her in Treacle Bumstead and I know I didn't see much of her after the age of nine when I was sent away, but she was the start of my life and I remember leaving her on that cold winter night and she warmed me with her smile and loved me even though she had a big brood of chavvies to keep her busy. She was the one I talked to when I made Marie pregnant and she was the one who understood what life was all about. Also, in 1973, my eldest daughter Debbie married Dale Tibbett, the top judo trainer in the country. He trained Brian Jacks, who was an Olympic bronze medallist and *Superstars* celebrity, and Dale used a judo club in Dunstable, which was just up the hill from Hemel. Dale was a black-belt and one of the UK coaches for the 1980 Moscow Olympics – my son Trevor had a go at the judo for a while, but didn't keep it up. He sparred with me one day and I was only used to the fists and not flinging my feet in the air and he ended up nearly knocking me out. I never fancied trying out judo again after that.

In the mid-70s, my brother Peter was working for a company from Leeds that did all the church work throughout the country, building new ones and renovating old ones. He got me on with them doing the brickwork and one of the churches we built was

Adeyfield Free Church in Hemel Hempstead. Now, I don't know if you'll remember, but the mid-70s were very hot – particularly 1976. It was scalding up on the scaffolding during the hot summer days and we decided to start work in the early morning as soon as we could see, sometimes in semi-darkness, and finish at 11:00 a.m., because it got too hot to go on and we had to take salt tablets to stop us dehydrating and falling over in a faint. We also built a church in Barnet and after that I took on ninety houses in Sunbury, so work was ticking over and things weren't too bad, despite the heat and hosepipe bans.

1977 saw the Queen's Jubilee year after twenty-five years on the throne and I could remember celebrating her coronation with a double ration of rum on the way out to Korea all that quarter-century ago. And I had to ask myself where the years had flown away to. I celebrated this time by streaking bollock-naked from the White Horse pub in Leverstock Green to the cricket club. About six of us did it altogether, me and three of the Daly brothers and a couple of others. The last man had to pay and it wasn't me. When we got there, we ordered up six pints of beer and the bar staff in the cricket club looked at us a bit sideways when we first streaked in, but I said, 'It's alright, we're celebrating the Jubilee and I'm wearing the king's new clothes . . . and so are all the others.'

So they served us. But the last man was naked when he arrived and holding no folding, so one of us had to walk back for his wallet. As it was my idea in the first place, I was the one elected to stroll back to the White Horse stark-naked and get the price of the pints. It's a wonder I wasn't arrested – but it was a nice day and people were in a goodish humour and pretended they could see the king's new suit.

Brothers Bill and Dave sold off my father's land in Newton Longville, where he planned to build 300 houses back in 1958, at a dirt-cheap price. I don't know why they did it, except that the company needed money – shortly after, the firm of F.W. Sears & Son Ltd went bankrupt. It wasn't through a shortage of work, but more mismanagement. The firm was working for the council at the time and was owed around £350,000. It was a lot of money to be waiting on and the financial strain was beginning to tell. Bill asked them for an ex gratia payment to keep things afloat, but they refused and the company went to the wall. The council said, after an investigation by the local newspaper, that they would have agreed to a payment if they'd been asked for one (which they were – and they refused). But there was a lot of big building firms in the area at that time and backhanders were flying about all over the place and who knows what deals were done behind closed doors. For all his faults, the old man would never have let it happen. The company was overextended by then and only making one per cent profit on every job, and Bill was conned by a man he used for pricing his projects, instead of doing it himself like FW would've wanted. But it wasn't for me to say – I was already an outsider.

I think it was about 1979 when I was moonlighting on this job up in Sawtry in Cambridgeshire, building an extension with my son Trevor and a few other boys. We'd go up there on a Friday and stay in the house over the weekend, and every evening after work we'd go a-boozing in a pub on the A1 called the Royal Oak.

I used to bring some pork sandwiches up with me that Marie made and she'd leave the crackling on so it made a crunching noise when I bit into it. I told the youngsters they were hedgehog butties and the crunching was the spines. I'd offer them around, but nobody ever accepted and it often put some of the boys off their grub altogether.

Sometimes we'd play cards when we got back from the pub, and one night Trevor got into an argument with another lad called Simon Jackson. Fists started flying and there was blood everywhere from a split eyebrow and a squashed nose. The man who owned the house didn't like all this aggressive commotion and the two boys got thrown out and told not to bother coming back. It was freezing cold outside in the late-winter night, so what else could I do but take it upon myself to get them safe home to Hemel Hempstead in my Austin A-40 motorcar. Now, I had that car for five years and never paid any road tax – I used to use the labels off beer bottles instead of tax discs, with the colour matching as near as possible the colour of the disc in that particular year. It'd be stuck up there on the windscreen and the coppers were never none the wiser.

Anyway, on the way back to Treacle Bumstead I ran out of fag papers, so I got Trevor to tear up some strips of the *Daily Telegraph* and I rolled my baccy in them. Thing is, the old newspaper made a lot of smoke inside the car and I couldn't see where I was going. I didn't want to roll the window down because it was brass monkeys outside, so I carried on down into the darkness. It wasn't long before we were pulled over by a couple of traffic coppers, probably lying in wait for some unsuspecting late-night farmer, along a remote stretch of the A1 near the village of St Neots. Now, the two boys in the car with me were covered in dried claret and I was using a label off a bottle of India Pale Ale as a tax disc. As well as that, a cloud of *Daily Telegraph* smoke nearly choked one of the coppers when I rolled the window down.

'Is this your car?'

'No, officer.'

'Who does it belong to?'

'Ray Hogg.'

'And where's this Ray Hogg?'

'He's dead.'

The traffic cop didn't know what I was talking about, but it was true. I bought the car from Ray Hogg a good while earlier, but he died before I could finish paying him for it so, technically, it still belonged to him. The copper leaned in the window and looked at Trevor and Simon.

'What happened to them?'

'Accident on a building site.'

'You taking them to hospital?'

'Yes, officer.'

'Where's all this smoke coming from?'

'The *Daily Telegraph*.'

He looked at me like I'd just escaped from some lunatic asylum and then he turned to his mate, who just shrugged his shoulders. It was late and I think they just didn't want the bother of breathalysing us and maybe having to drag us in and write up a report explaining how an Austin A-40 was running along on smoke from the *Daily Telegraph*. The desk sergeant would've breathalysed them instead of me. The copper leaned back in the window.

'You'd better be on your way, then.'

So I drove off with a trail of smoke flowing out through the window in my wake.

The irony of it was, back in Sawtry, there was only one policeman in the village and the station was just across the street from the Royal Oak. Sometimes when we'd come out after a skinful, we'd let his tyres down, and then call in an emergency from the public telephone down the road. We'd watch him come running out and jump into the cop car and then go mad kicking the car when he found out the tyres were flat. If the two coppers who pulled us over on the A1 knew anything about a pubescent prank like that, there would have been a bit more blood than what was stuck to Trevor and Simon, in the cells that night.

But the hand of fate took a turn, and about ten miles down the road the car ran out of petrol. We were in the arse-end of the Cambridgeshire countryside and it was too late to find anywhere open. It was like a fridge inside the motor, so God knows how cold it was outside. That's when we wished the police had arrested us after all – at least we'd have had a warm cell for the night. There was nothing else for it – we just had to sleep in the car. So we huddled down into our body heat and hoped the hypothermia wouldn't get us before the brightness of the morning.

I woke at 6:30 a.m. because the beer from the night before was reacting badly with my bowels and I had to find somewhere to do the business. So I took some more of the *Daily Telegraph* into a nearby field and squatted down. Unbeknown to me, a woman was out walking her dog and the next thing I felt was this cold nose nuzzling my bare bum. Well, I leapt half a mile in the air and let out a wild shriek that frightened the fleas off the dog and the wits out of the woman and the pair of them ran off a-howling across the field. I decided I'd better get out of there before the local vigilantes came a-hunting for the bald-arsed wild man who was terrorising their females and fox terriers. By the time I got back to the car, the boys had fetched some petrol in a can and we were on the move again.

It was Sunday morning and I decided to drive on the back roads the rest of the way home, so as not to get pulled by the police again. We ended up in the Alford Arms in the woodland village of Ashridge for the lunchtime session. The boys had a wash and brush-up in the public toilet and we were all singing and no hard feelings by the time the bell went.

What a lovely little life!

I think I've bored you enough with stories of building sites and bricklaying and stuff like that but, as we're on a sort of lavatorial subject, it was around 1980 when I was doing a bit of the plastering work that I'd learned from Mr Cheater in Verne Prison, down near suicide bridge in Highgate. The ceilings were very high in this house, so I set up a scaffold board across a couple of carpenter's trestles. Then I put two five-litre paint cans on the scaffold and balanced another board on top of them. I was trowelling away at the wall and humming a tune to myself and not minding much where I was standing, when the whole shebang tipped up and I came a-tumbling down and landed ribs first on one of the paint tins and squashed it flat as a flapjack. I decided to call it a day after that, but on the drive home my ribs were hurting bad and the steering on the car was stiff and the effort must have had some sort of detrimental effect on my sphincter muscles because, suddenly and without warning, I took an urgent need for a toilet.

There was nowhere suitable in sight except for a skip, so I left the motor and crept up beside it, squeezing the two cheeks of my bum together as I went, so as to avoid a nasty accident. I looked in the skip for a suitable receptacle, but all I could find was a ladies handbag. Needs must when the devil drives, so I did what I had to do and deposited the handbag back into the skip. As I was moving away in the motor, I caught sight of an old tramp in the rear-view mirror. He was reaching into the skip and what d'you think he pulled out? I pressed my foot down on the accelerator and was beyond earshot by the time he started screaming obscenities. I drove to the Swan in Pimlico and had fifteen pints of ale to sooth my frazzled nerves.

And I felt much better after that.

20

Saradakabowesyard!

I kept working away and my children grew up and left home and had kids of their own and me and Marie stayed married and loved each other just as much as the day we first met in the long room of the Goat public house in Berkhamsted, back in 1954. During the early part of the 1980s I was working as general foreman on a conversion job in Wheathampstead. We were turning Grahame Dangerfield's big old farmhouse – he was a TV wildlife personality like David Attenborough – into homes for the elderly. It was connected in some way to a cause that was sponsored by the Queen Mother, and the famous old farmhouse and listed building was turned into special flats. The job was done well and widely praised and an award was pending for all the major players involved, including my humble self – to be made to us personally by none other than Her Majesty the QM. Anyway, before the ceremony, I was driving my Jaguar XJ6, that I'd bought second-hand the year before, when I was stopped by an overeager traffic cop. I was reimbursing the bloke I bought the car from by instalments and he was holding the log-book until all the money was paid. The copper saw my tax disc was out of date and accused me of displaying it to deceive the police and asked me for the log-book, which I couldn't produce. In the end, I got charged with 'fraudulent conversion', whatever that means, and was hauled up in front of the beak at Luton Crown Court.

I pleaded 'not guilty, your honour' and my defence lawyer was a lady QC. Now, I have nothing against lady QCs, but this one was useless – maybe because I was on legal aid and wasn't paying for her services through the hairless nostrils. I asked her to cross-examine the copper who pulled me and ask him what 'fraudulent conversion' meant, but she wouldn't do it. She said it would just annoy the judge and make things worse. So I sacked her. I was found guilty and sentenced to 240 hours community service.

'I'm not doing it, your honour!'

The judge turned the same colour as jaundice.

'You can be sent to jail, Mr Sears.'

I knew if I broke a community service order, I'd be sent inside for three months. If I took the jail time, they could only give me the 240 hours, which was ten days. So, even though I swore I'd never go back to prison again, this was a matter of pride and principle and I took the custodial rather than risk breaking the community service order, which I had no doubt I would inevitably do.

'Very well. I sentence you to ten days.'

'Thank you very much!'

I was sent back to St Loyes Street in Bedford – the prison where James Hanratty was hanged for a murder he might never have committed in 1962. His grave was in a special part of the recreational area when I was there. While I was sticking up for my principles on the inside, the Queen Mother's award ceremony took place on the outside. John Laing, the famous architect, accepted the award of a cut-glass decanter on my behalf and apologised to the QM for my absence and told her I was 'on holiday'. I was sorry to miss meeting her because the Queen Mother was, of course, Colonel-in-Chief of the Bedfordshire and Hertfordshire Regiment, where I did my basic training, back in 1952. The cut-glass is down in Swindon with my daughter Heather.

Walking my daughter Heather up the aisle on her
wedding day, 23 September 1985

Marie got sick in 1988 and had to have her pancreas taken away. I looked after her and changed her dressings and tried to be her nurse and knight-in-armour as best I could. But I was still working and it was difficult to keep all the balls in the air and everything in its proper perspective. One morning, I saw the stitches had broken during the night and the skin had deteriorated and I could literally see inside her stomach, so she had to be taken back into hospital. When a pancreas is taken away, insulin isn't produced and has to be injected and Marie developed Type 1 diabetes. She was still smoking and emphysema soon followed the diabetes and her condition went from serious to something even worse. But she got a bit better and they sent her home again. I was still working when she came back out of hospital and I did all the housework and cooking and cleaning when I got home of an evening. But Marie got other complications, due to her condition – blisters came up on her legs and they'd burst and all the fluid inside would spill out like a pint of bad beer and I didn't know what to do. I'd panic when she hyperventilated and I had to test her blood on a little tab and give her insulin injections three or four times a day. I cut back my working hours to half a day so I could see to her needs more efficiently and eventually I had to get a part-time helper, because she was confined to a wheelchair and had to receive oxygen regularly.

I met the young lady they sent to help me in 1998 and she was detailed to come in and help around the house twice a week.

'Ken, this is Vicky. She'll be doing the cleaning from now on to give you a bit of a break.'

'I'll never remember her name.'

'Why not?'

'No good with names. I'll call you Slim.'

'Slim?'

'Because you're such a skinny girl.'

Slim has been with me ever since. During that fifteen years, she's brought up her family of two boys and a girl without their father and worked hard to do so, without much help from mainstream society. Slim doesn't resent how hard her life has been and always has a smile on her face when she walks through my door with the words:

'Hello, Ken, how's your week been?'

I have her coffee and hot sausage rolls waiting and she says, 'I do look forward to Wednesdays; it's the only day I get a breakfast.'

And if I wasn't such a cranky old codger nowadays, I'd ask Slim to marry me.

Thank you, Slim. For your time.

Marie was ill for fourteen years, from 1988 up to the time she died in 2002. She was on permanent oxygen twenty-four hours a day for the last few years of her life and I had to carry the hundredweight bottles the half-mile from Highfield chemist's to our house on my shoulder, because it was quicker than driving all round the houses to get there. She had all her mental faculties right to the end and she'd throw some bad language my way if I didn't do her dinner right. I used to say to her, 'I was once the boss in this house . . . how did this happen?'

The kids helped, of course, but they had their own families

and lives to lead and they did as much as they could. But it was mainly down to me to be her nurse and doctor. Marie continued to be in and out of hospitals and she was in West Herts local in Hemel Hempstead in October 2002. I had an accident at work while she was in there and fused the bottom two vertebrae in my spine and one in my neck and trapped a sciatic nerve for good measure. So I ended up in the same hospital as her. I was trying to get my story together before I saw her because I knew I'd get a going-over for not being more careful, but when I asked where she was, they said she'd been sent to a hospice in Berkhamsted – her home town. I went over to see her and we talked for a while until she got tired. I had to go back to West Herts for my own treatment and I left her alone at about 10:00 p.m.

Marie died just after midnight.

She wasn't a religious woman and was cremated at Amersham, after a heart-warming humanist ceremony. Later that night, when I was alone, I remembered when we got married and climbed into a bed together for the first time. She turned to me and said, 'My dream's come true, Ken. You're the love of my life from now on.'

I said back, 'You've taken my words from me, Marie. And we'll make this love last a lifetime.'

It lasted nearly fifty years.

And, as I write this, I find myself looking at her picture with the tears rolling down my face and fighting to find the words I always wanted to say to her. Words that might have gone something like this:

I just don't know how to explain the love I had in my heart for you, Marie. In all the years we were together, I was never able to really show how much you meant to me. It's eleven years since I lost you and the love is still so strong it hurts more than any physical pain I've ever endured and it will go on till I draw my very last breath. You look back at me from your photo and you know I couldn't show the weakness that was in my heart when you were ill. I had to be so strong, yet felt so helpless. When a man and a woman are as close as us, it's hard for one to live without the other and, when you died, my story ended.

I still love Marie.

And I miss her so much.

But I don't want to end on a sad note, even though there's not much left to say – not much more I want to say. In the new millennium year of 2000 the History Channel did a feature on my meeting with Marilyn Monroe in Korea and they gave me a £600 digital camera as a souvenir, but I didn't know how to work it and gave it away to one of my grandchildren. Brother Bill passed away in 2006 – he was waiting to have an operation on his leg and he died of blood-poisoning. I buried myself in my work after Marie and carried on in the building trade until I reached seventy-five. I remember doing a job for Vinnie Jones – he asked me to build a wishing well in his front garden in Redbourn. Vinnie was on television a lot in those days and he got some crew to come down and do a show about the well, which was pretty as a picture.

Well, I was drawing my pension then and when I saw the television crew coming up the lane with their cameras, I panicked in case the government might find out I was working and maybe I was breaking the law and they'd put me back in prison. So I packed up all my tools and scarpered. I found out later I could do a bit of work and earn a bit of extra bunce without breaking any ridiculous rules. Just an old hustler's hang-up, I suppose, from all the times when I was working the flankers.

People often ask me what I think about things today and I'm not sure if you'll want to hear my opinions – they might not be the same as your own and, if they ain't, I hope you'll indulge an old stick-waving reform school soldier. I always thought I was born a bit too late – the Roaring Twenties would've suited me more, with the jazz and the jigging and the drinking and devil-may-care – it was even better than the 1960s. I liked the 60s too, mind you, but those years weren't all they were cracked up to be. Maybe if you were a rich man's kid down in Carnaby Street or a pop star, but I was a builder with a young family out in the sticks. It was good on the weekends, when we went for a drink and the music was free and easy, but I never took no drugs, apart from when I was out foreign with the army, and my days of gallivanting with the women were over. So I wasn't swinging like I would have been if I was a few years' younger.

I'm not saying I'd want to change much about my life – I wouldn't. The way it always was with me is, what you see is what you get – and if you don't like what you see, then don't get too close.

Nowadays, most people have aerodynamic cars and full

freezers and televisions that talk back and mobile camera-phones and moleskin underwear and there's nothing wrong with all that stuff. But it seems to me it's all 'I wish I had this' and 'I wish I had that', and as soon as they get what they're wishing their life away for, they lose interest in it and straight away start wishing for something else. And the salesmen are at it all the time, no let-up, twenty-four hours a day – selling shit that nobody needs but everybody wants. And they all fall for it – they have to have this or that because the woman on the telly who acted in the Oscar-winning film says they have to have it – and surely they should trust what she says, above all people? And when they get it, it doesn't change their lives like they thought it would, so it has to be something else. It must be the thing the sports personality who won gold at the Olympics is selling! Look how happy she is – look at how happy he is – look how lovely they are. The stuff is already obsolete by the time they get it, so it has to be thrown away to make room for the next mach-20 model. And that's how the world evolves and revolves in these eager expansionism days. You'll say all this is just clichéd clap-trap and self-evident soapboxing and maybe it is – but I just wish the wallies who cut down trees to stop kids climbing them could see through the big con.

We should all be given our own little acre of land and let loose to grow our own grub and kill our own cattle and build our own boats and never mind listening to the hysterical screaming coming from the television screens.

I make my own sausage rolls!

The things most people rant on about in the pubs these days

are immigration and benefits and politics. Nobody much gives two tuppences for religion no more, except the fundamentalists, and I don't just mean the Muslims – the gunslingers and God-fearers are just as bad, if not worse. It's all a bucket of baloney and the only time I experienced real religion was with the angels in the Black Forest.

As far as immigration is concerned, we live on a small island here and we can't accommodate the rest of the world. But if conditions in other countries were improved, then nobody would want to come here, would they? Instead of exploiting those places, we should be helping to make them attractive to their own people, then there'd be no debate about foreigners and freeloaders and we'd have to do all the menial jobs ourselves. I'm sure that would suit a lot of soapbox shysters in this country.

Now, I have no particular axe to grind with the benefit system. We have to have a safety net to protect innocent children who slip through the television sales talk into the poverty pit. But I would take issue with some of the parents of these poor kids. You used to have to have a licence to keep a dog, but anybody can make a baby and then let somebody else be responsible for it after they've had their bum-bouncing night in the bed. I'm not saying people should be prevented from having kids, but if you bring a child into the world, then you're responsible for it until it's old enough to make its own way.

And I definitely think we should bring back hanging – not for murderers or molesters, just in case the judiciary might eye-for-an-eye some innocent bystander, but for politicians. Every politician should be strung up by the short and curlies in a town centre at least once a month. So we could shake our money back out of their pockets. Because they're an organised crew of bloody criminals and there's no difference between any of them. They're not left nor right, just centred – centred on themselves. You'll say this is throwing stones at the same old target and I suppose it is, but if we don't keep throwing the stones, the buggers will think they can keep getting away with mass hypnosis and metaphorical murder, like they do in America. Got to let them know there's still some of us who aren't hoodwinked by the sound bites and shamelessness and smiles-on-a-stick.

I went to see my doctor the other day and he asked me the same old questions:

'Are you still smoking?'

'Yes.'

'Are you still drinking?'

'Yes.'

'Smoking and drinking will kill you, Ken.'

'I know, doc, there's more people dying these days from standing outside pubs in the cold of winter, since you buggers brought in the smoking ban!'

And that's just one example of paper-shuffling oar-sticking interference in everything, trying to turn us all into politically correct clones. If smoking and drinking don't kill you, then the government will. And they're doing now to the NHS what they did to all the other institutions in this country, like the water and the gas and the railways. It's a basic tactic used by every political party in power before privatisation – starve the thing of money and, at the same time, turn it into a bureaucratic balls-up. After that they can say it needed to be saved by the private sector. Let me ask you something: do you think the water or the gas or the railways are being run better for being privatised? You'll only answer yes if you're a pocket-stuffing shareholder.

You're probably asking yourself by now, 'Has he not got a good word for anything in this twenty-first century?' And some things are better, like safety standards in the building trade. I wouldn't like to be back there now, mind you, with some jackass foreman shouting at me to wear a hard hat just because I'm standing on a manhole cover. But it's only right that building workers should be protected with safety regulations, just like workers in other industries. It's been a high-risk occupation for too long and these boys deserve to be able to go home at night without after losing a leg or an eye or half an ear. I'm sure there's many who won't agree with me, but that's always the way and I don't give a flying fiddle whether they do or not.

The modern army ain't the army of my day no more, neither. I won't say they're mollycoddled, with their bionic armour-plated flak jackets and their infra-red cameras and their computerised assault weapons – all a far cry from my days of Lee-Enfield 303s and poncho bivouacs and blisters. But I suppose if boys are going to be made targets of, so the shadowy super-rich can keep conning us, then they deserve a little consideration before they're killed.

There's only booze and women left to say something about.

The price of beer is killing off a lot of the old pub culture these days, that and these new gastro-places and theme bars – poseurs' paradises, with them all thinking they're so hippity-hop and drinking blue stuff out of bottles by-the-neck. But you can still find the odd proper working-man's pub, mostly on council estates and other areas not frequented by the fashionably fuzzy-eyed. And the beer can be kept longer these days than when it had to be pumped up by hand from wooden barrels – except, of course, if you drink the real ale. Nothing wrong with that stuff, but it can be a bit fierce if you're not used to it and tear the arse-hole off you in the morning and you have to clean the toilet with a hedgehog.

As far as women are concerned, I keep my love life to myself these days, if you understand. And I'll say no more about that subject.

So, I think I'll just end on that note. Oh, and I don't want no religious ceremony when I die. Neither do I want to be burned – just buried in unconsecrated ground.

And that's about it. All I can tell you now is:

Tiddymarkabanshew!

. . . as they say in the building trade, and if you don't like that, then:

Saradakabowesyard!

See you in the pub sometime!

Me and Marie at my daughter Heather's wedding, 23 September 1985